the

PSYCHIC
ADVENTURES

of DEREK ACORAH

DEREK ACORAH

Star of TV's
Most Haunted

the

PSYCHIC
ADVENTURES
of DEREK ACORAH

Llewellyn Publications
Woodbury, Minnesota

First U. S. Edition
First Printing, 2008
Originally published by Element, an imprint of HarperCollins*Publishers* in 2004

Cover art © Brand X Pictures (building), © PhotoDisc (texture)
Cover design by Ellen Dahl
Llewellyn is a registered trademark of Llewellyn Worldwide, Ltd.

Library of Congress Cataloging-in-Publication Data (Pending)
ISBN: 978-0-7387-1455-4

Llewellyn Worldwide does not participate in, endorse, or have any authority or responsibility concerning private business transactions between our authors and the public.

All mail addressed to the author is forwarded but the publisher cannot, unless specifically instructed by the author, give out an address or phone number.

Any Internet references contained in this work are current at publication time, but the publisher cannot guarantee that a specific location will continue to be maintained. Please refer to the publisher's website for links to authors' websites and other sources.

Llewellyn Publications
A Division of Llewellyn Worldwide, Ltd.
2143 Wooddale Drive, Dept. 978-0-7387-1455-4
Woodbury, Minnesota 55125-2989, U.S.A.
www.llewellyn.com

Printed in the United States of America

Dedicated to the memory of my beloved dogs, Cara and Bonnie,
who have now passed on to the world of spirit.
Until we meet again, girlies!

CONTENTS

ACKNOWLEDGEMENTS

I would like to thank all the people who have helped me on my not always untroubled pathway, especially Gwen, my wife, and Stuart Hobday, my long-suffering agent.

Without the help, support and assistance of these two people, I doubt whether I would still be working as a spirit medium today.

My gratitude goes to Karl Beattie and Yvette Fielding of Antix Productions, and also to Richard Woolfe of LIVINGtv for allowing me the platform to demonstrate my gifts to the wider television audience.

Finally, I would like to thank Patricia, Sue, Nicky, and Julie and all the other people who have constantly held their faith in me.

Introduction

As a small child I lived with my mother and my elder brother and sister at the home of my grandmother in Bootle, Liverpool. My father worked as a merchant seaman and was home for only very short periods of time. Gran's was a large three-story Victorian house on Brazenose Road, close to the then thriving port of Liverpool. After school each day we three children were sent up to the top floor to play whilst our evening meal was being prepared.

My first experience of spirit occurred one day just after Gran had called Colin, Barbara and me down for our tea. Being the youngest of the three, and with much the shortest legs, I was always the last to arrive downstairs. On this particular day, as I reached the first landing of the stair-case, I saw a man I didn't recognize. 'Hello, young tyke,' he said as he reached out towards me. It felt as though he had ruffled my hair. I was afraid because I thought that there was a stranger in Gran's house. Never had I reached the bottom of the stairs more quickly. I ran panting into the kitchen, shouting to Gran and my mother that there was a strange man in the house.

My grandmother and my mother hurried up the stairs, only to return a few moments later with bemused expressions on their faces. 'Tell me what the man looked like,' Gran said. On hearing my description, she reached for a tin in which old family photographs were kept. She took out a photograph and showed it to me.

'That's him!' I shouted. 'That's the man on the stairs!'

Gran looked at my mother and said, 'He's the next! Derek will be the next person in the family to work for spirit.'

I looked from my grandmother to my mother, not understanding what they were talking about. Gran gently explained to me that the man I had seen on the stairs was not in fact a stranger but my grandfather, who had passed to the world of spirit as the result of an accident three years before I was born. His name was Richard. 'In time, when you are older, Derek,' she said, 'you will see many people who have passed on to the next life. You will work with the people in the spirit world and will help many people on your life's pathway.'

I soon put all this to the back of my mind, but occasionally over the next few years I would recall the incident and question my grandmother about this 'world of spirit'. Each time she would explain to me that it was my destiny to work with the spirit people one day. 'But I want to be a footballer,'

I would tell her. 'I don't want to be a "gook"!' Gran would smile knowingly. All she would say was 'We'll see!'

At the age of 13 I began to realize my dream when I signed as a schoolboy player with Wrexham Football Club. I was happy. I lived, ate and breathed football. My bedfellow was not a teddy bear but a football, which I clutched to my chest as I fell asleep and dreamed of scoring goals for England.

At the age of 15 I signed as an apprentice-pro with Liverpool Football Club under the management of the great Bill Shankly, but sadly I didn't quite make the grade as a first-team player. After four years I moved back to Wrexham FC, then to Glentoran Football Club of Northern Ireland.

It was at this time that I met my first wife, Joan. After a season with Glentoran, I joined Stockport County FC, but didn't feel particularly happy with my footballing career. Joan had just given birth to our son, Carl, when I was asked by the players' union in Manchester whether I would be interested in playing football abroad. The idea appealed to me and after a lengthy discussion with Joan, I agreed. We were Australia bound! I joined USC Lion of the South Australia Football League.

Unfortunately, although I was very happy living in Australia, Joan was not. She missed her friends and her family back home. The physical rigours of the game were also beginning to take their toll on me. Ultimately, we made the decision to return to England. By 1982 my footballing days were over.

Throughout my career as a professional footballer I had not lost my interest in the world of spirit. There had been many instances when spirit people had made their presence felt and impressed upon me proof of survival after this earthly life. With my return to English shores came the time for me to start working for spirit.

Sadly, my marriage to Joan had come to an end. Now living on my own, I began to do private readings for people in my home, but soon the demand became so great that I had to find office space. Although I was working as a full-time spirit medium, I had not yet developed the gift of clairaudience. This was about to change.

Ever since my grandmother's realization that I was the one who had inherited her mediumistic gifts, she had gently tutored me and explained to me the workings of the spirit world. She taught me that we all have spirit guides and that I was no exception. Throughout my lifetime many guides would come and go, she explained, but my main guide was a black man from the Ethiopian regions of Africa and he would never leave me. One day he would introduce himself to me.

One evening I was at home alone. I had just completed my evening meditation and was sitting listening to some music. Suddenly I heard a voice saying, 'Hello, Derek.' This was repeated four times. Then the voice said, 'I'm Sam.'

Even though I was perfectly well aware that I was alone, I looked around, expecting to see somebody. There was nobody there. Realization dawned—at last my spirit guide had spoken to me! The words my grandmother had uttered all those years ago had come true.

It was during these early days that I met my second wife, Gwen, who had herself been through the sadness of a marriage breakup. I knew immediately upon meeting her that she was somebody who would understand me; we had a bond which remains unbroken to this day.

We moved to a home just outside Southport on Merseyside and as well as my private readings I began to work as a regular guest on a number of radio stations.

I was driving through to Liverpool one day when my mobile phone rang. It was Gwen ringing to tell me that the Granada Breeze television programme *Psychic Livetime* had been in touch to ask whether I would be interested in making a guest appearance. This was the first time that I had been offered a spot on a television programme. Nervously, I agreed.

The following Friday I arrived at the Manchester studios and was introduced to the presenter of *Psychic Livetime*, Becky Want. 'Hi, Derek,' she said. 'Now what we're looking for is somebody who can read tea leaves.'

Tea leaves! It was National Tea Week and one of the producers of the programme had decided that it would be a good idea to get a psychic in to do a tea leaf reading for Becky. I was nervous. I had not conducted a reading using this method before, but as the introductory music began, Sam told me to relax, that everything would be fine and that he wouldn't let me down.

The time passed quickly. I conducted Becky's reading successfully and before I knew it she was thanking me and telling me that what I had told her was correct. The closing music was playing and it was the end of the programme. 'That was wonderful, Derek,' Becky said.

On the Wednesday of the following week I received another telephone call from Granada Breeze, asking me whether I would like to join them again the next Friday. The public response to my initial appearance had been so great that the producer thought it would be a good idea if I were to appear weekly. I was delighted to accept. So began my career as a television psychic.

Since that day I have had many adventures. From the relative obscurity of local radio and appearing on a minor satellite television channel, I have been catapulted into the public eye on a much grander scale—all thanks to Karl Beattie and Yvette Fielding, who invited me to take part in LIVINGtv's celebrated *Most Haunted* programme.

It is almost three years now since the pilot programme was filmed and we are preparing to shoot the fourth and fifth series. Now I find that I am communing with spirits from different eras, from different backgrounds and different cultures. I have taken a journey into the history of my homeland—something which I sadly neglected to do during my schooldays. For the first time in my life, I have been frightened; for the first time I have sometimes been perplexed at the workings of spirit. What I have not lost, however, is my faith in the world of spirit. The spirits have never let me down.

In this book I have attempted to give an insight into my experiences whilst travelling the country, both on stage and in front of the television cameras. I hope that you will enjoy making that journey with me.

✓

First Steps

$\mathcal{S}$oon after I had met Sam, my work for spirit increased. My first experience of stepping up onto the platform in a Spiritualist church was a particularly memorable one.

Gwen and I had driven to Blackpool. It was a hot sunny day and as we headed out of the seaside town we heard on the car radio that the motorways were terribly congested, so we decided that we would delay our departure in order to miss the heavy traffic. To while away a couple of hours we thought we would take a trip farther up the coast to Lancaster.

We arrived in the old town around half an hour later. By now it had started to rain, so our original idea of taking a walk around the town did not seem nearly so appealing. I drove around looking for a parking space and found one in a narrow side street. As we sat wondering what to do next to kill the time, I happened to look through the rear-view mirror and saw a small building behind me. Over the door were the words 'Lancaster Spiritualist Church'.

I got out of the car, walked over to the notice board and saw that the service would be commencing in 15 minutes. We attended the Spiritualist church in Liverpool regularly, but I thought it might be nice to join the service in Lancaster. Gwen agreed.

We walked through the door and squeezed into a couple of seats at the rear of the hall. It was very small, with a capacity of no more than 50 people. The presiding medium for that day was a lady named Gloria Duthy. I had heard of Gloria, but had never seen her work.

The service began with the usual prayers, hymns and dedications before the medium took the platform. Two or three messages had been passed on from loved ones to members of the congregation when suddenly Gloria pointed to the back of the hall and said, 'I've a man here. He's a very brusque Scot and he wants to speak to Derek!'

Gwen dug me in the ribs with her elbow, but as I have no Scottish links in my family and as Derek is not the most uncommon name, I remained silent.

'I know I'm going to someone at the back of the hall with this man,' Gloria said. 'I want the Derek who was linked to football! This spirit man is telling me to tell Derek that "the boss" is here and he's still putting the goals in the "onion bag" over there!'

Now I knew that the message could only be for me. 'The boss' was most definitely my old boss from my footballing days at Liverpool Football Club, the legendary Bill Shankly. He was the only person I knew who referred to the goal net as 'the onion bag' and it would be far too much of a coincidence to have two Dereks in such a small congregation who both had links with football and the great man. I put my hand up.

'Thank you, Derek,' Gloria said. 'This man is telling me that you shouldn't worry about not making it to the top in football. He tells me that you'll make your mark in another way—working for spirit. He's saying that you must never give up, that you must continue on, no matter what obstacles are put in your way, because you are meant to do this work. He's telling me that you should be up on this platform conducting the service. He tells me that I'm good but that you will be better. He's laughing and saying, "Just tell him it's Shanks!"'

Gloria continued with messages from my grandmother Helen, my Uncle George and a family friend called Micky. She told me that one day my name would be in lights and that I would work for spirit in all parts of the world, and finished by asking me if she could talk to me after the service.

When the final prayers and hymns had been completed and the absent healing requests read out, I waited at the back of the hall to speak to Gloria. She was a lovely lady and congratulated me on the work that I was to do for spirit.

After a few minutes the booking secretary for the church approached us. 'I'd like to book you to conduct next week's service here,' she said.

'*Me?*'

I was overwhelmed. Although I had spent many years as a member of a Spiritualist congregation, I had never taken the platform before. Gwen was busily digging me in the ribs, urging me to agree. She had always said that I should have more confidence in myself. I reluctantly agreed that I would travel to Lancaster the following Sunday to take the role of presiding medium for their evening service.

For the whole of the following week I was extremely nervous and wasn't looking forward to our trip to Lancaster at all. Finally the day arrived. We set out to travel along the M6 but as we were nearing the service station at Charnock Richard, the car began to overheat. We pulled onto the forecourt and checked the radiator. Although there was no sign of a leak, there was very little water in it.

'I think we'd better telephone the church and tell them that I won't be able to make it,' I said to Gwen.

'No way,' she replied. 'You've said that you'll take the service and you'll do just that, even if I have to push you there in the car!'

We filled a couple of bottles with water and set off once more. We had to stop twice to let the engine cool and to top up the radiator, but eventually we arrived in Lancaster and parked up in front of the church.

As I walked in through the door my stomach was rolling and I was feeling terribly nervous. The walk to the podium seemed endless as I tottered along on quaking legs. Then the prayers were said and the hymns were sung and before I knew it, it was time for my demonstration of mediumship.

'Please don't let me down,' I begged Sam.

'Don't worry, Derek, this is your destiny,' Sam replied.

And I need not have worried. After a faltering start, the messages began to flow. I saw spirit people and I heard spirit people, and they all passed on messages of love to their family members sitting in the congregation. I found I was really enjoying myself.

Before I knew it I was being called to time by the president of the church. I received a round of applause and my heart swelled with gratitude. As I stood there on that tiny platform in one of the smallest churches I have ever been in, I knew that I had been foolish to question spirit. Those on the other side knew that I was ready to undertake platform work—they had told me so through Gloria—but I, through human frailty, had doubted it. Thank goodness that Gwen had an unswerving faith in my mediumistic abilities and had urged me to do just what Shanks had told me—to carry on no matter what obstacles were put in my way!

'PEOPLE FRIENDLY' SPIRITUALISM

Over the following years I travelled the country appearing in Spiritualist churches in different towns. Although I very much enjoyed this aspect of my work for spirit, it frustrated me that so few people were attending the churches. At the very best, we could only expect an audience of 50 or 60 people. In those days people had some very strange conceptions regarding Spiritualism. They imagined the churches to be places where only a few rather strange people gathered to hold séances in a darkened room with a red light glowing. The hard and fast belief was that 'normal' people just did not go there, only people who wanted to 'talk to the dead'. I realized that it was time that Spiritualism took a step forward into the present day and become more 'people friendly'.

I knew that the great Doris Stokes and one or two of the better-known mediums in the UK had appeared in theatres. 'What would happen,' I thought, 'if I did something similar, though obviously not on such a grand scale?'

With this idea in mind I contacted one or two cabaret clubs in the Liverpool area to see whether they would be interested in hiring out their premises to me for an evening of clairvoyance. Unsurprisingly, I received a number of point-blank refusals, but eventually I received a positive response from the manager of the Orrell Park Ballroom. A date was arranged and a month or so later I was waiting backstage to be announced to an audience of 250 or more people.

'This is the way it's meant to be,' I thought to myself. 'If I'm to be working for spirit, surely it's part of my job to ensure that I spread that knowledge to as many people as possible.' I knew that I had been inspired to make the correct decision.

It was the first time that I had demonstrated to an audience of more than 40 or 50 people. Word had got around from people who had been for private sittings with me and Gwen had kindly offered to print off some leaflets advertising the event and had trudged around the streets of the local area putting them through the letterboxes. This was a task she undertook on a regular basis for subsequent evenings of clairvoyance at venues throughout Liverpool, though her endeavours came to an abrupt end one day when a rather sneaky dog failed to announce his presence by barking, but silently waited under the letterbox and bit the ends of her fingers as she pushed the leaflet through!

That first evening at the Orrell Park Ballrom I began my demonstration with a short talk and then proceeded to approach people in the audience and give them messages from their loved ones in the world of spirit. Time after time I was met with tears of joy and gratitude from the people to whom I spoke. It was a wonderful feeling. At the end I received thunderous applause and I knew that the evening had been a great success. 'This is the way it's meant to be,' I thought to myself...

Following the success at the Orrell Park Ballroom I decided to move further afield. Over the next year or two I appeared at civic halls and small theatres. Audiences were growing and interestingly I noticed that they were no longer comprised exclusively of women. I also began to notice that other mediums were following in my footsteps. The word of spirit was definitely being spoken to a wider audience now!

A Breeze

$\mathcal{T}$ime moved on and eventually I was spreading the word not just in theatres but also on television. One day early in 1999 I was arriving at the *Psychic Livetime* studios when I was stopped by Rachel, one of the assistant producers. 'Derek, can you please help me? I've lost my engagement ring. I don't know how or where and I'm so upset. Not only is it my engagement ring, but it's irreplaceable because it's an antique.'

Rachel was dreading having to tell her fiancé about the loss. She had spent hours searching all the rooms she had been into since arriving at the studios, but to no avail. The ring was nowhere to be found.

I closed my eyes and asked Sam to help. I was shown a room full of clothes with dummies dressed in different costumes. This was all rather strange because I knew that Rachel was an assistant producer and would spend her days in the gallery or on the studio floor and not in the wardrobe department. Nevertheless, I decided to ask her whether what I had been shown was correct. She stood and thought for a moment and then remembered that when she had arrived for work that morning she had taken a telephone call from the wardrobe department asking her to send a runner up to collect an outfit for the presenter Becky Want. She realized that as it was still very early, none of the runners would have arrived at work, so she decided that she would go and collect the items herself. When she arrived at Wardrobe, she was directed to an outfit hanging on a rail in the corner of the room.

'Whilst you were there, did you do anything else in that room?' I asked. 'Because I feel you were looking for something else and that is when the ring slipped off your finger. My insight is that if you return to the wardrobe department you will find your ring underneath the rail on which Becky's outfit was hanging.'

With that I had to go and get changed and go over to the studios where the programme was to be filmed. I was very busy for the next few hours, but at the end of the filming, I came out of the studio to see Rachel waiting for me. She was smiling broadly and twiddling the fingers of her left hand in front of my face. On the third finger was her engagement ring!

'You were right, Derek,' she said excitedly. 'I went back over to Wardrobe and I found my ring lodged in some clothes which were directly under the hangar which I had taken to Becky. Thank goodness! I had completely forgotten about going over to that department. In fact I think it's the only time I've ever been over there in all the time I've worked for Granada!'

All's well that ends well!

Before Rachel walked away she said to me, 'Oh, Derek, I nearly forgot! The editor wants to see you.'

This was most unusual. I wondered what on earth I was being summoned to the office for. At the end of the programme I walked over to Dean Street rather apprehensively.

As I entered the editor's office, she was smiling. 'Come in, Derek. We've some good news for you.' She went on to tell me that because of the popularity of *Psychic Livetime* it had been decided to create a new programme which was to be named *Predictions*. People would be brought to the studio to demonstrate the various disciplines of mediumship and I would be given the opportunity to demonstrate my mediumship to a live audience in the studio.

I was absolutely delighted. This would be a first for British television. I felt honoured that I was to be the first medium to appear regularly working with a studio audience.

THE ISPR VISITS THE UK

*T*he International Society for Paranormal Research (ISPR), headed by Dr. Larry Montz, is based in Los Angeles, California. Dr. Montz has been a paranormal investigator for over 27 years. His speciality is field parapsychology. Early in 1999, at his invitation, I had taken part in team investigations of various sites in Hollywood. (These investigations are fully documented in my first book, *The Psychic World of Derek Acorah.*)

After my return to the UK Dr. Montz kept in constant contact with me and one day in March he phoned to tell me that the ISPR team would be travelling to the UK. They had teamed up with Dotted Line Entertainment and were coming over to conduct several investigations and make two videos.

On a breezy day in April the team arrived at Heathrow airport. It was wonderful to meet up with them all again. Dr. Montz, Daena Schmoller, Linda Mackenzie, Shawn Roop and my good friend Peter James wearily walked into the arrivals hall and we were soon excitedly discussing the first of the locations they intended investigating the following day—the Jack the Ripper murder sites.

JACK THE RIPPER

The East End of London in the late nineteenth century was one of the most disreputable areas of the city and the Whitechapel district was witness to a series of horrible murders. It was to be the job of the ISPR team to uncover the identity of the murderer, who was known only as 'Jack the Ripper'.

Donald Rumbelow, historian and Ripper expert, was invited to join the team on their investigation. Although Jack the Ripper has been 'credited' with the murder of six women at different locations, we would be visiting just two of those murder sites. It would be Donald's job to authenticate any information the team members might produce.

The first place the team was taken to was Mitre Square. Today this is a pleasant flagged area where people may sit and enjoy a sandwich during a summer lunch break. Along one side of the square runs a schoolyard in which children play. However, the cheery sounds of a lunchtime game of football faded as I concentrated on opening myself up to the energies of the infamous events which had taken place over a century earlier.

I allowed myself to drift back in time. The April sunshine disappeared as the square darkened and it became nighttime. It was quiet, though I could hear shouting and

merriment coming from a nearby hostelry. A woman's raucous laughter echoed out of the darkness. The name 'Catherine' came into my mind. Clairvoyantly, I could see a woman
dressed in dark shabby clothing. Wisps of greying hair could
be seen straying from underneath a greasy bonnet. She had
the raddled features of somebody who is no stranger to drink.
I knew that she was a victim of the infamous Jack the Ripper
and that Catherine was her name.

As I allowed myself to come forward to the present, I
noticed a bench not six feet away from me. I walked over and
touched it. 'This is the spot!' I shouted to Dr. Montz. 'This is
where Catherine's life was taken from her.'

Although the bench had been placed in the square at a
much later date, I was able to use it to pick up on the residual energies of the woman's dying moments. I could feel the
dread and heart-stopping fear she had experienced. I was
overcome by the stench of blood and something which I
could not describe but which was horrible and offensive. I
could also tell Dr. Montz that Catherine had not been the
first of this vile creature's victims. By the time he met her,
Jack the Ripper was a seasoned killer.

As I stood contemplating the spot, I became aware of
another name. 'Lily—Elizabeth!' I said. 'She was a victim
too. There were two killings and both on the same night!'
I could sense the slashing of the victims' bodies as they
were disembowelled and butchered.

Donald confirmed that on the night of 30 September
1888 both Catherine Eddowes and Elizabeth Stride had

fallen victim to London's most famous serial killer. He had viciously killed and brutalized their bodies.

Then Donald guided us to another area. He stopped at a place called Durward Street. 'This was Buck's Row,' he told us and stood back expectantly waiting to hear what we had to say.

I allowed myself to drift back in time once more. The small area of rough ground where I was standing bore no resemblance to the picture which unfolded before my eyes. Now it is a concrete jungle with high-rise flats and flagstones sprouting tufts of grass. There is a graffiti-scarred concrete garage next to a fence with a wooden gate hanging off its hinges.

I was drawn to this break in the fence and as I walked over to it I could smell the same revolting odours which had assaulted my nostrils in Mitre Square. This time I could see the body of a rather stocky dark-haired woman; her clothes were obviously filthy but appeared to be soaked in blood. Her face was slashed and I could see that one of her ears was hanging off. In stark contrast, on the floor not far from her body lay what appeared to be a shiny black straw hat. I was impressed to utter the name 'Nicholas'. Could this be the name of the murderer? The name 'Polly' was also strongly evident to me.

As I allowed myself to drift back to the present day, I relayed the picture I had seen to Dr. Montz and Mr. Rumbelow. They confirmed that it was in the area of the gateway that the body of a woman called Polly was found.

'Can you describe the person responsible for the murders?' Dr. Montz asked me.

'I feel that there were two people responsible,' I said. 'I believe that there was a "copy cat murder". The man responsible for most of the murders is tall and slim—not heavy-set at all—and in his thirties. He has strong crease marks down the side of his face with high cheekbones. He has dark hair with touches of grey to the sides and he definitely has facial hair. He carries a pocket watch and seems to be constantly conscious of time. He certainly isn't a poor working man. The person I'm talking about is used to mixing with the aristocracy and I feel he could have some connection with royalty.'

'And a name?' questioned Dr. Montz.

Sadly, no. On this occasion I was not being impressed by the name of the man who became infamous as 'Jack the Ripper'.

I would like one day to revisit the site of the Whitechapel murders and see what else I can uncover. I still maintain that more than one person was behind what I would describe as ritualistic killings. I feel that five of the murders were carried out by the same man but there was at least one other murder for which another individual was responsible.

THE EUXTON MILLS HOTEL

Following our investigation of the killing fields of Jack the Ripper, we travelled north and based ourselves at a hotel in Leyland, which is a suburb of the old Lancashire town of Preston.

The Euxton Mills Hotel is a 300-year-old establishment which was once a coaching house which accommodated travellers on their journeys from Scotland and the north of England to more southern areas. The manager, Keith Burgess, had kindly agreed to allow the ISPR team to conduct an investigation of the premises. Although Mr. Burgess was sceptical of mediumistic abilities, he was interested to see whether the ISPR team could shed any light on the strange goings-on experienced by members of his staff.

Immediately as I walked into the lounge area I was aware of a spirit man standing in the centre of the room. Wearing a dark cloak and stovepipe hat, he had the appearance of a Victorian gentleman. He said nothing but as he gently faded from my view Sam told me that his name was George Chapman and he had frequently visited the hostelry and enjoyed his stays there. He was a jovial soul who enjoyed the company of women and had a tactile nature. Indeed, to this day, employees of the hotel talk of being touched by an unseen person.

As the spirit form of George Chapman disappeared, Linda, Peter and I were simultaneously drawn to the washroom area at the rear of the lounge and in particular to the ladies' toilets. As I entered the toilet area I had the feeling that things were not quite as they should be. It was a ladies' toilet but I felt a distinctly male influence and that George would have visited these facilities when he arrived at the hotel in his earthly life.

At that moment, the temperature began to drop dramatically and a lady in a long Victorian-style dress and hat walked past and through us and exited through the door into the lounge. She seemed intent on what she was doing and appeared to be keeping a very tight hold of a small bag. I was not given her name nor was I told the reason for her continuing to visit the hotel, but it was confirmed by the staff that a 'grey lady' is often seen in the ladies' toilet area.

Our investigation continued in the cellars. I was immediately aware of a male presence and knew that the male in question was not the jovial George Chapman. This was a different personality—not angry, but certainly mischievous.

'You have problems down here,' I said to Keith. 'In particular I feel you have problems with the beer lines. There's spiritual interference here. A man comes down and plays with the lines and I feel you could have experienced the gas in the kegs pushing back.'

Keith laughingly confirmed that on many occasions he had experienced just that and had been forced to go up and change his shirt because of the soaking he had received.

'Well, the next time it happens, tell Tom to stop it,' I advised.

I had the distinct impression that Tom had at one time worked at the public house and was still jealously guarding what he considered to be his domain.

TONGE HALL

Tonge Hall in the Middleton area of Manchester was built by the Tonge family in 1594. It is a beautiful Tudor-style black-and-white building and is owned by Norman Wolstencroft, who was our amiable host for the next investigation.

The main room of Tonge Hall, where Norman was seated with our expert for the day, Mr. W. John Smith, was cosy and welcoming after the cold and rain outside.

I had only been standing in this room for a few moments when I became aware of a gentleman. 'I have a man with me,' I told Dr. Montz, 'and he wants to talk to me. He tells me his name is Richard and he's very proud of his staircase! He's asking us to follow him!'

We all hurried out, following Richard as he took us out of the lounge and past a staircase to a part of the house which was undergoing renovation. 'There,' Richard said, pointing towards a set of stairs which the team had been unaware of, 'these are the stairs that I designed and I'm extremely proud of them!'

Mr. Smith, our expert, confirmed that Richard Tonge had indeed built a second staircase and noted that this set of stairs was unusual for the time in that they were built out of wood.

'There are two men here now,' I said, 'both Richards! They're different generations. One is very much younger than the other. And there's a William too—he has a very bad limp. William seems very fond of the younger Richard.'

Mr. Wolstencroft was able to confirm that William was the father of the younger Richard. He had received a bullet wound to his leg in the First World War but wouldn't allow amputation, so he spent the rest of his life with a limp. He also told us that his grandmother had five sons. Four of them were wounded but Uncle Dick had been particularly badly hurt and also limped. This must have been the Richard who had shown himself to me earlier.

We were all drawn to the upper levels of the old house and all felt compelled to enter one particular bedroom. As soon as the door was opened I immediately became aware of a young girl, eight or nine years of age, with red hair in plaits. Almost simultaneously Linda and I said the same name: 'Ann!'

The child seemed afraid and upset. I felt that she had passed to spirit as the result of an illness, certainly not as the result of an accident or anything more sinister. Nevertheless, she seemed to be frightened.

Suddenly there was a huge drop in the temperature in the room. The reading on the gauge which Dr. Montz was holding decreased dramatically and Linda and I became aware of a male presence who seemed to be more malevolent than the kindly souls we had experienced earlier. He was not at all pleased at our being at Tonge Hall. Linda, a gifted and experienced healer, attempted to calm the spirit, but he was not going to be so easily placated. Dr. Montz's electromagnetic field metre needle swooped backwards and forwards. I stood next to Linda. I knew that it would take the strength of both of us to send this unpleasant spirit man on his way.

Suddenly, Linda stumbled. 'He pushed me!' she shouted. Dr. Montz and I grabbed at her arms to steady her. We were at the top of a steep set of stairs and the last thing we wanted was for Linda to go tumbling down them. I braced myself and moved forward towards the entity. Too late I realized that I had allowed him to get too close to me. I felt as though the wind had been knocked out of my lungs and I doubled over coughing and choking, fighting desperately for breath.

Slowly I managed to stand upright once more. As I did so, I saw the outline of the angry spirit man fade and disappear. He had warned us! He was not going to allow us to interfere with his home!

We were all completely shocked at what had happened. Meanwhile, little Ann was still standing in the bedroom.

She had not moved and seemed to be waiting for us to help her in some way. 'She's lost,' Linda murmured. 'She needs to be sent to join her mother in the light.'

We turned and looked through the doorway to the bedroom across the hall and straight over to a window through which could be seen the dying rays of the April sun. Through that window I could see a lady, very peaceful and calm, with her arms outstretched towards Ann. Linda and I mentally took Ann by the hand and led her towards the lady who would take her into the light of the spirit world and eternal peace.

Norman was later to explain that his father had a sister named Ann who had succumbed to a childhood disease at the age of eight. She had red hair and long red pigtails!

LIVE AT THE LIVERPOOL EMPIRE

The day which I had long awaited had finally arrived. Tonight I was to be appearing for the first time at the famous Liverpool Empire theatre.

As I would be conducting a demonstration of clairvoyance and mediumship for two hours, it was decided that the rest of the ISPR team would carry out an investigation of the theatre without me. I am happy to be able to report that they were able to confirm the presence of the spirit of a girl aged approximately 12 who had fallen from the front of the circle onto the seats of the stalls below. Linda and Peter confirmed that she was an active presence and the names 'Joanna' or 'Jessica' were suggested. The spirit of this young girl is frequently seen in the corridors, front of house and stalls of the theatre. She is reported to be very pretty with long blonde hair and is dressed in Victorian-style clothing. She is often seen in the company of a man with either black eyes or no eyes. Unfortunately, on the day of the investigation, the spirit man chose not to make the team aware of him.

Meanwhile I was honoured that Julie Goodyear had graciously agreed to introduce me to my audience at the beginning of the show. I had worked with Julie briefly whilst she hosted the Granada Breeze programme *Psychic Livetime* and was delighted to see her once again.

I had a tremendous evening and judging by the audience's response, so did they. Many people think that a demonstration of mediumship is all 'doom and gloom' with an atmosphere of misery and sadness. This is not the case at all. If a person had a cheerful and outgoing personality whilst here on Earth, they will carry that personality through to their life in the spirit world.

I can recall one hilarious moment at the Liverpool Empire when a young man from the spirit world tapped me on the shoulder and told me that he'd like to speak to his sister Karen and her friend, who were sitting in the audience. 'Tell them Carl wants to speak to them,' he announced in his cheeky Scouse accent.

I duly did as requested and a gasp went up from a young lady who was sitting half a dozen rows back in the stalls.

'I'm alright now, our kid!' shouted Carl. 'Look!' And he proceeded to skip across the stage.

'I can't do that,' I said to Carl.

''Course you can, Degsy,' came the cheeky reply.

'Carl's telling me that he's fine now in the world of spirit,' I told Karen, 'and he's kicking up his heels just to prove it.'

Carl continued, 'It wasn't any good, that stuff. I knew I shouldn't take it, but it got a hold of me and I just carried on. Didn't think it'd see an end to me, though. But guess what? I'm not skint over here—you don't need money!' With that he turned out his pockets. 'And I don't have to keep looking over me shoulder!' He burst into peals of laughter and ran across the stage, warily looking over his shoulder. 'I don't need to keep an eye out for the rozzers over here!'

I looked out to Karen in the audience and wondered how on earth I was going to pass that message over. 'Oh well! Go for broke,' I thought and repeated exactly what Carl had told me, giving a demonstration of the turned-out pockets and the hasty scuttling across the stage whilst looking over my shoulder.

Karen and her friend were beside themselves with laughter, together with the rest of the audience. 'That's our Carl,' Karen said. 'He was always getting into trouble and had to keep on his toes.'

Carl's message continued. 'Seriously, though, kid, I'm OK over here, and guess what? I've met old Uncle Jimmy! He's shown me the ropes. Tell you one thing, though, I'm not happy about our Dave nicking me bedroom!'

Karen laughed through her tears. 'Dave's our brother and when we lost Carl, Dave took over his bedroom. Their tastes in decoration weren't quite the same,' she added tellingly.

Carl passed on messages of love to his mum and dad and the rest of the family. He finished up on a light note by telling his sister that the medium she'd been to see just after his passing had not been able to make contact with him. 'Because she was no good, that's why,' he scoffed. 'Next time you want to speak to me, go to somebody who can do the bizz!' Karen nodded her agreement.

The evening was drawing to an end, but there was just one more thing to do. Dr. Montz came on stage to ask whether any member of the audience who had experienced spirit activity in their home would agree to the ISPR team visiting their premises to conduct an investigation. The reason behind his request was to prove to sceptics that an investigative paranormal team could go into an undocumented building and still pick up on the spirit activity there without the possibility of research.

A number of people put their names forward, but one young man stood out as being more in need of our assistance than the others. To preserve his and his family's privacy, I have changed their names.

Paul had come to the theatre in the hope that he would receive a message from his wife Paula who had passed to the world of spirit just five weeks before. She had suffered from that horrible condition called cancer. Paul was absolutely bereft. He had been left to look after his small daughter Jemma on his own as his family lived out of the Liverpool area.

We arrived at Paul's neat home in a suburb of Liverpool the following morning. Paul was there with his daughter and his mother. Dr. Montz felt that I should be the first person to go into Paul's home to speak to him.

I entered the house by myself, leaving the rest of the team outside. I walked over to Paul and took his hand. I could feel all the hurt, sorrow and desperation that he was experiencing. I picked up the anguish of his loss.

Jemma was there, clinging to her toy rabbit. She had become destructive since the loss of her mother, and her family was worried about her. As I did not want to conduct a reading or any sort of investigation in front of the little girl, I asked Paul's mother to take her through to the kitchen area of the house, together with Linda Mackenzie, who has an amazing empathy with children and has marvellous healing powers which I felt could benefit Jemma.

As I stood in the lounge I became aware of a slim young woman in spirit. She smiled gently and said, 'I'm Paula. This is my home and Paul is my husband.' She pointed over to the window and told me, 'That was my last resting place—there under the window.'

'Did you have Paula's coffin at home?' I asked Paul. 'Because I have a young woman with me who's telling me that she was laid under the window. She's also telling me to thank you for the necklace you put around her neck whilst she lay in her coffin.'

Tears welled up in Paul's eyes. He told me that he had placed a cross and chain around Paula's neck as she lay there.

'You've heard Paula around the house, especially on the stairs,' I said.

Paul confirmed that he had indeed heard noises, especially on the stairs. The noises were reminiscent of when he used to help Paula up the stairs when the ravages of her illness had made it impossible for her to climb them herself.

'There's something serious I need to speak to you about,' I told Paul. 'You mustn't do what you've been thinking and planning. Paula's telling me that you must carry on. You must stay to take care of Jemma.'

Paul gasped and as he stared up at me, I could see the tears welling once more in his eyes. 'I know what you're saying, Derek,' he said as he stared down at his hands. 'I understand.'

'Always know that Paula loves you,' I told him. 'She wants you to be happy. She knows that it will take time, but you must persevere because you have to be responsible for Jemma.'

We went into the kitchen where Linda was playing with Jemma. I could see the healing colours surrounding the child and I knew that Linda had been sending out healing energies whilst playing with the little girl.

I like to think that we were meant to visit Paul's home and that as a result of our visit he was able to continue on and come to terms with the passing of his young wife. I feel that he learned that life does indeed continue beyond physical death and that loved ones never really leave us. They remain with us until we ourselves leave the physical plane and rejoin them in the world of spirit.

BELGRAVE HALL

The grand finale of the ISPR team's visit to the UK was a visit to Belgrave Hall in Leicestershire. Belgrave had recently been in the news around the world. The cctv system at the old hall had picked up some anomalous footage.

Had a ghost been caught on camera? The video footage purported to show two ghostly apparitions on the gravel path to the rear of the hall. The ISPR team had been invited by Leicester City Council to view the tapes and to visit the hall in an effort to determine whether it was true ghostly activity or a mere fault on the videotape.

It was planned that the team would arrive at midnight. Dr. Montz asked each member of the team to enter the hall individually so that he could compare findings.

I was the third team member to take part in the investigation. As I entered the rear pantry and walked through to the dimly lit kitchen I was aware that there was indeed spirit activity within the hall. I continued through to the hallway and was surprised to find that my nostrils were assailed by the smell of freshly baked gingerbread and the sweet smell of cooked fruit. 'How odd!' I thought. I would have expected such smells to have been apparent in the kitchen, but not in a hallway.

As I was mulling over this strange situation, out of the corner of my eye I noticed a movement on the staircase that led up to the first floor. A smell of freesias became apparent and there on the staircase stood the spirit form of a lady. She was in her mid-fifties, had white hair and was dressed in a deep red Victorian-style dress. She said nothing, but drifted slowly up the stairs and disappeared onto the landing above. I was strongly impressed to utter the name 'Alice' or 'Ellis'.

'This is one of the Ellis sisters,' Sam advised me. 'She loved her home and her garden and loves to come back and visit. Although the furnishings have changed, she's very happy that her home still remains and that she's able to come back and pay visits.'

I reported to Dr. Montz what Sam had told me about the lady. As I followed her spirit form up the staircase, I was drawn to a room which was full of the paraphernalia of children: small chairs, a cradle and one or two low arm-chairs. As I entered the room I could feel a definite temperature drop. 'Annie's here,' I said. 'She was a nurse-maid or nanny. She was very proficient and had very strong links with this building. She's talking sadly of the loss of two of her small charges. I feel that these two children were lost to spirit through consumption. They're buried in the churchyard.'

I moved from the nursery and into one of the large bed-rooms. Here I encountered a man in spirit. He was quite old and bent over. Although there was no communication from him, I gained the distinct impression that he had been some type of servant and that he had worked long and hard for his master.

As we moved from bedroom to bedroom, although I was very aware of the residual energy contained in these rooms from the many years of occupation by various families, no further spirit people showed themselves to me.

I descended the stairs once more and entered the drawing room. There in the corner I could make out the spirit form of yet another lady building up. I knew that she had been a good and sensitive person in her earthly life.

'I'm Eliza,' she told me in direct communication. 'I lived here with my sisters.' She talked of her sister Isobella who had a leg impediment. She was very sad that she had not been able to enjoy walking around the beautiful gardens of Belgrave Hall, though she laughingly added, 'She has no problem now!'

It was time for the whole team to congregate in the hallway. Stuart Warburton, curator of the Belgrave museum, had joined us and was confirming our findings with Dr. Montz. It was now 3 o'clock in the morning and we were all becoming more than a little weary.

Suddenly we all became aware that the temperature had plummeted. I knew that we had been joined by another past inhabitant of Belgrave. I also knew that unlike the other people in spirit that I had encountered here, this spirit entity was not at all pleased at our intrusion. 'Edmund,' boomed a voice in my ear. 'Edmund Craddock.' I had feelings of agitation and negativity. The other members of the team confirmed that they too were picking up similar feelings. We all agreed that this man definitely did not want us in his former home. He was a forceful personality who was blustering and huffing, but because there were four experienced mediums present he was unable to cause problems. It was to be a different story three years later when I visited Belgrave Hall with the crew of LIVINGtv's enormously successful programme *Most Haunted* and Vic Reeves and his wife Nancy Sorrell.

Now the ISPR investigation of Belgrave Hall drew to an end. Dr. Montz had analysed the videotape footage and had questioned each of the team about it. We all agreed that though Belgrave Hall has many ghostly visitations and an enormous amount of residual energy, what had been caught on tape was nothing more than a combination of bad weather and a camera fault which had given the impression that a ghostly apparition had been photographed when in fact it had not.

And so the ISPR team's visit to the UK came to an end. The following day I waved them off from Heathrow airport and wondered when we would meet again.

In fact it was the following July, when I flew across the Atlantic to meet the team for the premier showing of *Ghosts of England* and *Ghosts of Belgrave Hall* at the Vogue Theatre on Hollywood Boulevard.

THE JAMES WHALE SHOW

y now I was well used to working on radio and had been a regular guest on Radio City's *Billy and Wally Show* each Friday for over a year. I had also had a regular Sunday-evening guest spot on Red Rose Radio when I took telephone calls and gave live readings on air.

But in September 1999, just as my first book, *The Psychic World of Derek Acorah*, was due to go into the shops, I received a telephone call asking me to go to London to guest on the Talk Radio *James Whale Show* and my heart plummeted! James Whale! James has a reputation of not suffering fools gladly and I had the distinct impression that he would definitely consider me to be a fool.

On the appointed Sunday Gwen and I drove down to London. To say that I was nervous would be an understatement. We arrived at the studio and as I took the lift up to the reception desk I could hear James's voice being piped through the corridors. 'And my guest this evening is Derek Acorah. He says he can talk to dead people!'

'Don't worry,' Gwen told me. 'Just promote your book and we'll be out of here in half an hour. It's not as though he's going to eat you!' I hoped she was right.

Before I knew it I was sitting in the studio with James. 'Welcome, Derek,' he said. 'Now tell me—just what exactly is it that you do?'

I proceeded to explain my work as a medium. 'Right!' said James. 'Then perhaps you wouldn't mind doing a reading for me?'

'Oh dear!' I thought. This was the last thing that I had expected to do. 'Don't worry, Derek,' I heard Sam whisper.

I opened myself up to James's vibrations and saw a lady in spirit who came up behind him and stood there smiling. She was quite plump but gave me the impression that she had not always been so, that once she had been lithe and slim. She impressed upon me that she had had lots of problems with her hips but that she had passed to spirit as a result of cancer. She mentioned the name 'Michael'. Then she was joined by a gentleman who also stood behind James and placed a hand on his shoulder. I got the distinct impression that this man loved the open air and had some links with farming. Oddly enough, though, I also saw him standing behind a bar in the role of landlord.

All the time that I had been passing this information over to James he had said nothing, only uttering the odd grunt now and again. When I finished speaking he was gracious enough to confirm that his mother had once been a ballet dancer but had ended up with hip problems because of her dancing and consequently had put on weight.

She had passed to the world of spirit as a result of cancer. The name 'Michael' was certainly relevant. He was James's father, who had been the landlord of a public house for many years, but whose desire had always been to buy a farm and live off the land. I breathed a sigh of relief. Sam had not let me down.

'Would you like to stay on after the midnight news and take some telephone calls?' James asked. Of course I would!

Before I knew it, it was 2 o'clock in the morning and James was bringing his show to a conclusion. I had been on air for three hours, including two hours of telephone calls. James was jubilant. 'Well done, Derek!' he said. 'We'll have to have you back!'

And so after that every Sunday evening would see me travelling to Stockport for a live link-up with James in his London studio. For three hours I would conduct telephone sittings live on air.

At this time I was continuing to conduct my personal readings as well as joining Billy and Wally on a Friday morning on their Radio City show. I was also appearing every week on Granada Breeze television in Manchester. The demands on my time were so great, I didn't even have time to arrange theatre appearances. 'You need an agent,' James said to me one day. 'I know a great one. He's my own agent. I'll give you his number.'

A few days later I contacted Stuart Hobday. What Stuart thought on that day I really do not know. His background lay in music and theatre. To be contacted by a clairvoyant must have seemed a little strange to him, but thank goodness that he agreed to meet me. We have worked together successfully ever since and I would like to think that this situation will continue for a very long time to come.

My weekly spot on *The James Whale Show* unfortunately came to an end in the April of the following year when James had to undergo serious surgery. Since then I have been a guest on his show whenever my schedule has allowed, but I often look back fondly to that day when two panic-stricken people drove to London to meet the great James Whale.

PREDICTIONS WITH DEREK ACORAH

All things psychic were now proving to be hugely popular with television audiences and *Livetime* had changed its name to *Psychic Livetime* and was now solely involved in airing mind, body and spirit subjects. The producers decided that another programme should be created, called *Predictions*. Guests would be invited to the studio to demonstrate their expertise in the various aspects of mediumship, astrology, dream analysis and so on. My contribution would be to demonstrate mediumship to a small studio audience and to conduct one-to-one sittings live on air.

The show was pre-recorded, but what was filmed went out on air—what the television audience saw was what had really taken place. I was elated when I was told that the viewing figures for *Predictions* were as great as, if not greater than, the figures for *Psychic Livetime*.

Predictions continued for approximately 12 months and at the end of that time I was called in to see the editor once more and was informed that the format of the programme was to be changed and it was now to be called *Predictions with Derek Acorah*. The response to my contribution had been such that the producers had decided to dedicate the programme to me alone. I was surprised but elated, because I now knew that I was indeed fulfilling my destiny, just as Gran had predicted all those many years ago.

In the new programme I would continue to demonstrate mediumship to a studio audience, but there would be a new feature which would involve me going out to meet people and conducting sittings for them in their own homes. A further section of the programme would see me being taken to alleged haunted locations to conduct investigations there. I would not be told where I was going or the name of the location I was to investigate.

I had mixed feelings about this. Although visiting people to conduct sittings for them held no fear for me—it was what I was used to and I loved my work—the idea of wandering around old buildings talking about days gone by held no appeal whatsoever. I had hated history at school and had always managed to escape history lessons to train for my school football team. Needless to say, my school reports always demonstrated my dunce status where history was concerned! Nevertheless, I agreed to take part in the programme. With Sam's help, I knew I could do it.

SAMLESBURY HALL

The first place I visited was Samlesbury Hall. Samlesbury is a small central Lancashire town which lies between Blackburn and Preston. The manor itself is a black-and-white building which was built in the fourteenth century after the original hall had been burned by Robert Bruce when he raided Lancashire.

What surprised me most as I entered the old hall was the sound of girlish laughter and I had the definite impression that this had been an educational establishment at some time. The name 'John' was impressed upon me. 'John Cooper,' I said.

No sooner had I uttered that name than the energy around me changed and I felt as though I was in an inn. Once more there was laughter around me, but this time it was accompanied by the smell of ale and roasting meats in the huge fireplace. The sensations were only brief and were quickly replaced by a more sombre feeling—a feeling of desperation and despair. Then I heard a loud bang! 'Somebody shot themselves here!' I said. I could not say who it was, as I was not being given a name, but I knew for certain than somebody had committed suicide.

I went further into the premises. The name 'John' rang out again. It was not the same man whose residual energy I had picked up on earlier. This was another man and as I watched I could see him building up in front of me. 'Sir John!' he said. 'Sir John Southworth!'

I knew that this man had been a good man—quiet and peaceable—but I also knew that he had suffered because of his faith. There was another sadness which he had experienced in his life too. The name 'Dorothy' was whispered. I felt the urge to move to the upper floors of the building. Up we went, past the priest hole and on to a bedroom. 'Dorothy!' the name came again. I had the impression of a tragic young lady, a murder and horrendous grief. 'Her brother murdered her betrothed,' said Sam. 'It was an accident. He and his two companions were murdered by Dorothy's brother. She went mad with grief!'

On the investigation went, out into the gardens and back into the hall again. Before I knew it the producer was telling me that our time was up and that we would have to vacate the hall. I was disappointed. To my surprise I had enjoyed wandering around the old manor house and meeting the inhabitants of years gone by!

SOMETHING MISSING

Another part of the programme involved me visiting people in their homes to conduct readings for them. The television audience was invited to telephone or write in, a name would be drawn at random and then I would be taken to that person's home. I met hundreds of wonderful people this way and everybody was extremely kind to me. I look back fondly to all the people I met, but once there was one little boy I was more than happy to help.

Paul was aged two and Sylvia, his grandmother, had written in to ask for a reading. Her daughter-in-law Jane had passed to spirit and her son David had been left to look after Paul on his own. As David was a long-distance lorry driver, he had sold his home and moved back to live with his mother so that she could care for Paul whilst he was away.

Jane had been gone for three short months and during that time Paul had been quiet, morose and cried each night when he was put to bed. Sylvia knew he was missing his mother but thought there must be something else that he was missing too. She could not have been more correct.

As I entered Sylvia's home I immediately became aware of a young lady in spirit. She was slim and dark-haired and I gained the impression that when in her physical life she had been a joyous soul with a bubbly sense of humour. 'Yes, that's Jane,' Sylvia confirmed. 'She was always laughing. She didn't have a care in the world.'

Jane then told me herself that she had loved her life here on Earth, that she and David had been very happy and were planning another baby. 'Life couldn't have been better,' she said. 'The trouble is, I just didn't see them coming!' She had been coming home from a friend's home one evening when a car had mounted the pavement and struck her. After two days in hospital she had passed on to the spirit world. She told me that her father Jim had been there to collect her and that she was at peace, but she still missed David and Paul very much.

'I inspired Sylvia to contact you,' she continued. 'There's a problem with Paul. He's missing his toy elephant. He always used to have it with him in bed at night, but when David moved to Sylvia's house it was packed into a box and it's still in there.'

I turned to Sylvia and told her what Jane had said. 'I didn't know anything about a toy elephant,' she told me. She walked over to a cupboard under the stairs and took out a large cardboard box full of cuddly animals. After rummaging around, she finally pulled out a blue velvet elephant.

On seeing his toy, Paul let out a shriek of glee. He toddled over to Sylvia, took hold of the elephant and clutched it to his chest.

'I haven't seen him looking so happy since Jane went,' Sylvia said. 'Just wait until I tell David.'

A day or two later the studio received a telephone call from Sylvia thanking us for coming to her house and telling us that Paul had gone to bed each evening without a problem now that he had been reunited with his long-lost friend.

NO SMOKING

One of the funniest incidents on the road occurred when the film crew and I had travelled to Northumberland to conduct a reading for Jean, who lived in a quaint village some 40 miles west of Newcastle-upon-Tyne. We were booked to spend the night before in a small hotel which was actually located on Hadrian's Wall. Rain had fallen relentlessly for the whole of our journey north. By the time we reached the hotel, which was situated down a farm track, the stream which ran alongside it had burst its banks and we were forced to drive through a foot or more of water to reach our destination.

Weary and damp, we eventually drew up outside the picturesque establishment. As I walked through the door I noticed that everywhere I looked there were 'No smoking' signs. As I am rather fond of my cigarettes, I wondered where I would be able to have one without causing a problem.

The owner of the hotel was a rather brusque, no-nonsense character and as she showed us up to our rooms I nervously asked her where I could smoke if I wished to do so. 'Out on the fire escape!' came the sharp answer.

I looked through the window. It was still pouring with rain. 'Maybe I'll wait a while,' I thought to myself. I wasn't that desperate!

After leaving my bag in my room I wandered back to the lounge to meet up with the crew and discuss the plans for the following day's filming. As I sat in an armchair I became aware of a man in spirit. He seemed a jovial character and though he did not communicate with me by voice, I knew that he was in some way connected to the building and the woman who owned it. The air suddenly became full of the rich aroma of pipe tobacco. 'Hmm,' I thought, 'so the lady doesn't allow smoking, but it doesn't stop this chap!'

A couple of minutes later the crew joined me and I told them about the visit from the man in spirit. As we were talking, the proprietor appeared. She sniffed the air and looked accusingly at me. 'You've been smoking in here,' she snapped. 'I told you that there's no smoking allowed on these premises. My father used to smoke and I hated it!'

'But I haven't been smoking!' I spluttered. I tried to explain to her that her father had paid a visit to the hotel and that it was in fact he who had brought the smell of tobacco. I explained that one of the easiest ways for people in spirit to bring their presence to our attention is to permeate the atmosphere with a well-remembered smell. It may be a wife's perfume, the scent of a grandmother's favourite flower or even, well, the distinctive smell of tobacco.

'And you expect me to believe that!' the woman snapped. 'I've told you—no smoking inside. If you want a cigarette you can go out onto the fire escape.'

Feeling thoroughly dejected, I took myself out into the elements to share an umbrella and a cigarette with one or two of the crew members, who were giggling uncharitably at my discomfiture.

'Never mind, Derek—you can't win 'em all,' said Steve the cameraman.

I've taken the blame for many things in my life, but I didn't ever think that I'd be blamed for the smoking habits of a ghost!

INVESTIGATIONS

Over the next 18 months or more I would be taken to a number of sites in Lancashire and Cheshire to conduct investigations for *Predictions with Derek Acorah*. We even travelled as far as Edinburgh on one occasion. I had not visited Scotland's capital city before and was fascinated to learn that apart from the beautiful buildings such as Holyrood House, Edinburgh castle and all the other wonderful old buildings which make up the Royal Mile, there was a darker and more sinister city underground.

AULD REEKIE

A trip to the Edinburgh vaults is not for the faint-hearted. At the entrance to Auld Reekie vaults there is a museum full of medieval torture instruments. It was a sobering start. Devices such as thumbscrews, jaw breakers, tongue removers and flesh-tearing instruments filled me with horror as I imagined the agony suffered by the victims of the witchfinders all those years ago. Would I have been brave enough to suffer for my beliefs, or would I have taken the coward's route and not have admitted my ability to communicate with the spirit world? It has not been on my spiritual pathway to incarnate into that era, so I will never know.

We climbed down the stairs to enter a passageway eerily lit by dim green-shaded lights on the walls. I could just make out a number of chambers, each with an arched entrance. I walked to the end of the passage and entered the first chamber. It was empty. I could detect nothing of significance there, just the residual energy of people who had called these dark caverns their home. It was surprisingly warm. I had expected a damp, dark atmosphere, but this was not the case.

I moved on into the next chamber. It was different here. I knew that there was spirit presence. I became aware of a young girl in spirit. She stood in the corner of the room and seemed to be cowering into the corner. She was no more than 13 or 14 years of age and was dressed in a drab brown dress which appeared patched and dirty. She had been a serving girl who had been brutally treated by her master until she had succumbed, as had many of the dwellers of this underground city, to the plague which had ravaged the area in the eighteenth century. She did not communicate with me, but through Sam I was able to establish the dreadful circumstances in which she had lived her physical life. I asked Sam to help the girl to move on to the light of the spirit realms.

On entering the next chamber I was surprised to be met by the feelings of activity. I could smell liquor and could hear clairaudiently the sounds of barrels rolling and being opened with a sharp rap to the bung with a long-gone hammer. A grey-haired man in gaiters, wearing a leather cover over his front, was going about his business of selling ale to his subterranean customers. The sound of drink-fuelled raucous laughter and merriment echoed around. It was so loud that I glanced at the crew members. I was sure that they must also be hearing the sounds of yesteryear, but no, the cameras were rolling and nobody was giving any sign of being aware of the noise I was hearing.

'Can you hear that?' I asked.

'Hear what?' came the response. 'Just keep talking, Derek. It's all fascinating stuff!'

We entered a couple more of the chambers, but again, apart from the residual energy in the fabric of the walls and ceilings, no spirit activity was evident.

The next chamber we came to, however, was very different. This room contained a circle of stones and I knew immediately that this area had been used by people who had been dabbling in what is commonly known as 'the black arts'. Hatred and malevolence hung heavy in the air. The area had to be cleansed. If it was to be left in its present state no good would come of it and anybody of a sensitive nature would suffer upon entering the room. I could pick up from the atmosphere that people who dealt in devilish activities had used this area in an attempt to summon negative entities to further their dark practices.

'I always knew this place was no good,' said our guide. 'I always had a feeling that something bad had gone on in here.'

As my time was limited and I was unable to conduct a cleansing myself, I extracted an assurance from him that he would approach a local medium to do the job.

THE HUNTER'S TRYST

The Hunter's Tryst, our second location, had been home to the Six Foot High Club and was reputedly haunted by the Devil in person. Unfortunately (or perhaps fortunately), although I conducted a thorough investigation of the old inn I could find no trace of anything remotely devilish. I did communicate with a lovely lady in spirit who had at one time been the landlady of the public house and I even solved the problem of items going missing in the kitchen—it was down to the playful spirit of a young boy who had once worked there—but the Devil, I'm afraid not! The loud bangs, moans and groans that were being heard were due to nothing more than airlocks in the pipework.

CRAIGMILLAR CASTLE

The following day saw our arrival at the final destination, Craigmillar Castle, which lies approximately three miles from the centre of Edinburgh. Although missing many of its roofs and in parts semi-ruinous, Craigmillar is one of the most perfectly preserved late medieval castles in Scotland. It was to be the first time that I had investigated a castle and I was unsure of what to expect.

We entered through a doorway in the curtain wall and walked across the grassy expanse to a gateway which opened on to the inner courtyard. It was an extremely windy day, but the moment we entered the courtyard, which dominated by a huge tree, all was peace and calm.

I felt the atmosphere was charged with the residual energy absorbed over the centuries.

As I entered a doorway and turned to my left I detected no spirit activity but was aware of the memories of great household activity. I was impressed by the name 'Preston'. The names 'William', 'John' and 'Simon' were also strong. As I turned to retrace my steps back into the courtyard, I had the definite impression of two large hunting dogs brushing past me.

We wandered around, going from room to room, and although I gained many impressions of life from the times when the castle would have been the bustling hub of Scottish society, I detected no spiritual presence. Yet as we moved from place to place, I gained a picture of life as it would have been. I was aware that royalty was no stranger to these castle walls. There had been regal visitors here. For the first time I felt the essence of the woman I was to become familiar with over the months of my investigations with *Predictions*: Mary Queen of Scots.

In the dungeons I picked up on the agonies suffered by unfortunate souls who had spent time there. As I ran my fingers over grooves gouged into the stone doorway, I felt the despair that they had experienced.

We continued on until we reached the top of the castle. It was time to walk along the battlements. The wind had gathered in strength and it was almost gale force as I stepped out onto the ancient stones. As I walked unsteadily along, I saw the spirit form of a lady approaching me. Surprisingly, she was not attired in the medieval costume that one would imagine in a castle of Craigmillar's age, but in 1920s fashion. She wandered along the battlements, seemingly impervious to the wind against which I was battling. As she approached me, she pointed down towards the grounds, where I could see a small graveyard. 'Patricia' came the name. As she moved on I turned around to watch her retreating back. As she reached a point approximately ten feet away from me she disappeared just as suddenly as she had appeared.

Craigmillar Castle is a fascinating place and I enjoyed my visit enormously, though I was most disappointed that my first visit to a castle had been so short on spirit activity. That is not to say, of course, that the spirits do not visit; it merely means that at that time they chose not to make themselves known to me.

TUTBURY CASTLE

My first visit to Tutbury castle was also with a crew from Granada Breeze television. On our arrival at the car park we were amazed to be met by a gentleman dressed in the full regalia of a cavalier. He bowed low in greeting as he swept his velvet feathered cap from his head. 'Greetings and welcome to Tutbury!' he called out.

Tutbury castle holds themed weekends and at that time Stephen was involved in organizing them. He had thought that it might be a good idea to meet us in character that day!

Stephen directed our cars down the pathway, through John of Gaunt's Gate and on to the front of the house. As I gazed across the lawns I was taken back in time. Instead of a broad expanse of grassy lawn, I could see many people going about their daily business. There was the bustle of village life, with children playing, wives cooking meals and the men conducting their trades—woodworkers, butchers, cobblers, and so on. Dogs slunk around in the background, looking out for scraps of food. Small carts creaked along the hard-packed earth roadways and I could see a few cattle underneath the castle walls grazing on sparse grass. I brought myself back to the present day. There was work to be done.

Turning to look at the door of Tutbury castle, I was amazed to see none other than Mary Queen of Scots standing in the doorway leading to the Great Hall. I blinked rapidly a few times. This was no spirit form, but Lesley Smith, curator of the castle, in the flesh. Lesley's portrayal of Mary Queen of Scots is remarkable. I was to hear her make a speech later that day in the guise of the tragic queen which moved me beyond words.

Our investigation was to begin in the Great Hall. As I opened myself up to the vibrations of this imposing room I became aware of the spirit form of a man building up.

He had a regal bearing. I knew that I was in the presence of royalty.

'Describe the man to me please, Derek,' demanded Lesley.

'He's very short,' I told her, 'with almost elfin features. He has long hair and a pointed beard. I definitely feel that he was a royal personage in his physical life.'

'What's he got on his feet?' asked Lesley.

I looked down to the footwear of our regal spirit visitor. 'Shoes,' I replied, 'but they have a high heel on them.'

'You can only be describing Charles I,' Lesley told me. 'Is there anything else?'

'Yes! He's walking over to the fireplace. He is putting his arm up and leaning against the fireplace. I get the definite impression that he is very proud of something to do with the fireplace.'

'You're right, Derek,' Lesley said. 'Charles I built that fireplace!'

I continued to wander around the room. Sitting in an enormous chair in the corner, I felt that this chair had been occupied by many people over hundreds of years, some of them royal, some not. There were so many vibrations. As I sat there I began to sense the presence of a woman in spirit. I just knew that we were in the presence of the real Mary Queen of Scots. Although she did not show herself I could feel her emanations around me as I sat on that chair.

'Mary Queen of Scots—I feel she is drawn here because of your portrayal of her tragic life,' I told Lesley. 'I'm sure that she is an inspiration to you when you give your speeches.'

'I agree with you, Derek,' said Lesley. 'I often feel that Mary is around me and almost talking through me when I speak.'

I knew that Lesley's feelings were correct.

I rose from the chair and walked over to the staircase which descended directly from the Great Hall.

'There's something mysterious about this staircase,' I said to Lesley.

'It was discovered not more than a couple of years ago,' she told me.

I looked down the stairwell. At the bottom I could see a male spirit form. He stood silently looking up at Lesley who was standing at the top of the staircase with both her hands leaning on the balustrade which prevents people from accidentally falling down the stairs. From nowhere a gust of wind came rushing up the staircase. Lesley's head-dress and heavy black velvet gown blew dramatically.

'There's a man down there who isn't particularly pleased by our presence here,' I told her. 'I'm not being given his name at the moment but he's not at all happy!'

We moved into a small ante-chamber next to Lesley's private office, which leads directly from the Great Hall. At that time the room was empty of furniture, apart from a table holding catalogues. There was a small fireplace on one wall and in the corner was a wooden staircase to an upper floor.

As I walked into this room I was drawn to the corner opposite the doorway. I held out my hand. I could feel the sudden drop in temperature in this corner.

'Put your hand out and feel how cold this area is,' I invited Lesley and the crew.

Each person put their hand into the area I had indicated and exclaimed at the difference in temperature.

'This is a cold spot,' I told them, 'a vortex where spirit entities enter and leave our atmosphere. If you wish, you could think of it as being a spiritual doorway.'

I turned my attention to the staircase. I asked Lesley if it would be possible to go up to the rooms overhead.

'Of course,' she said, 'but there are only a couple of storerooms up there. The doors are open, so go ahead.'

I climbed the stairs and turned the knob on the door to one of the storerooms. Nothing happened. I tried a few more times but still the door remained firmly shut. Steve, the cameraman, tried to turn the knob, but he had no more luck than I did.

'I don't know! Men!' rang out Lesley's voice from below. 'Let me come up and open it for you!'

I gave the doorknob one more try. I knew that there was somebody in spirit who did not welcome our visit to the room. Suddenly the door flew open. Steve fell back in shock, almost stumbling over. I looked into the room and there in the corner stood the spirit man I had last seen standing at the bottom of the staircase leading into the Great Hall. 'Get out of here!' he demanded. 'This is no place for you! I command that you leave this place!'

'And who are you?' I asked him.

'Who am I? You dare to ask who am I? I am Edmund!'

He drew himself up to his full height and stood there with an imperious expression on his face. He seemed unwilling to continue speaking, but pointed towards the door. Although no words were exchanged, I could feel the strength of his anger building in the atmosphere. I took a step back towards the door. I knew that if I stayed in the room his anger would grow. This could cause problems for me and the crew.

I descended the stairs. 'There's a very angry man up there,' I told Lesley. 'He says that his name is Edmund.'

'Ah! That's the Earl of Lancaster,' she told me. 'He wasn't a very nice man at all.'

I could believe it. I was rather shaken by the venom he had displayed. He certainly resented my intrusion into what he considered to be his own property.

I decided that I would go outside for a few minutes to clear myself of Edmund's vibrations. As I walked along the pathway I saw a white peacock standing next to the path. As I approached, its tail rose in the classic display and it nodded its head to me. As I stood admiring the magnificent bird, I felt peace and calm wash over me.

It was time to continue the investigation. I felt drawn towards an area of the lawn in front of the house. 'There are bodies buried here,' I told the crew, 'lots of bodies. I'm not sure exactly where, but I know that somewhere near here there are the physical remains of many people!'

Time was growing short and there were still so many places to visit. A decision had to be made as to where our last investigation would be. I chose the chapel and the north tower.

All that remains of the chapel are the foundations and a depressed area in the ground. I walked over to these ruins. I said nothing, but felt as though I should be searching for something. I started to poke around amongst the ruined brickwork.

'What are you looking for, Derek?' asked Lesley.

'I'm not sure,' I replied, 'but I know that something was lost and I'm being impressed by a lady in spirit—at this moment I'm not sure who, but I know that she lost something which she valued.'

'Wait a moment,' said Lesley and she disappeared off in the direction of the house. On her return she held her hand out to me. On her palm was a ring. It was obviously a very old ring, as its design was quite primitive.

'This ring was found in the ruins of the chapel,' she told me. 'I've never felt happy since it was taken from where it was found. Its owner is obviously looking for it. I'm going to return it to its hiding place. Maybe then the spirit of the lady can rest easy knowing that she has her property back.'

Now came the climb up the many steps to the top of the north tower. Up we trudged. I was leading the way. We were about halfway up when I felt a rush of cold air passing me. Liz the researcher and Jan the producer both let out screams. 'Something just pushed past us, Derek!'

What they had felt and what I had seen was the residual energy of a soldier, complete with sword, rushing down the narrow winding stone staircase. This was not his spirit form, but the memory of a journey down the stairs which he had no doubt made on numerous occasions. This memory energy would be replayed time and time again and has no doubt been experienced many times by many people.

It was time to leave Tutbury. As I turned to say goodbye to Lesley I told her, 'Mary Queen of Scots will appear again. She will be seen here very soon on the ramparts.'

'I hope so, Derek,' said Lesley. 'It's been seven years since she was last seen at Tutbury. It wasn't a happy place for her. I'd given up hope of her ever being seen here again.'

A few weeks later Lesley and her husband Christopher came to the Granada Breeze studios in Manchester on the day that the Tutbury castle investigation was to be included in the *Predictions* programme.

'You were right, Derek,' Lesley told me. 'Mary did appear on the battlements at Tutbury and she was seen by a number of people!'

CLAIRE SWEENEY

C was at the studios in Manchester recording *Predictions with Derek Acorah* when an assistant producer approached me to tell me that Claire Sweeney of *Brookside* fame was waiting to see me.

I was so pleased. I had been conducting readings for Claire for a number of years, charting her progress ever since she was a young girl and her mother used to visit my offices in Liverpool for readings. When Claire reached the age of 17, she would come along herself to consult me. I had told her in those early days that she would work as an entertainer on cruise ships and that one day her name would be in lights.

This time as I greeted Claire I said to her, 'You're going to think I'm crazy, but I've just seen you presenting a programme where the general public will be put to certain challenging tests. If they fail to complete the task, you'll have to take the challenge on for them!'

Claire said she couldn't see herself ever doing a programme like that.

'Oh, but you will,' I told her. 'And you'll be moving home quite soon. I've just seen you carrying a couple of bags into a house. It's a big white house. There are other people in this house.'

Claire told me that she was not planning a move at the moment and certainly would not consider sharing with other people. I knew that she lived in Liverpool and was very close to her mother and stepfather. We both wondered why I would have seen something like that. I was mystified and Sam was not being very helpful by telling me any more. It was only many months later, after Claire had taken part in the Channel 4 programme *Celebrity Big Brother*, that she telephoned me and reminded me about my prediction involving 'a big white house' which would contain other people.

My next insight involved Claire on a very big stage. I could see her dressed in a beautiful dress. She was moving around the stage, dancing and singing. There were other people on the stage with her. I knew that London's West End featured strongly in this. 'Claire, you have to sing, sing, sing! I can see you making an album. Your voice has to be heard!'

'Well, it'd be lovely if it were to happen,' she replied.

I was very excited for Claire. She had worked hard from a very young age and although she was a successful actress I knew that in her heart she yearned to make her name on the stage and in music.

My reading for Claire continued and covered her emotions. I will not divulge the content of this reading through respect for her privacy. I am pleased to see, however, that she has all the happiness that I would wish for her and I know that it will continue. And I was delighted to hear later on that my predictions for her had proved to be accurate.

CORONATION STREET

As I was leaving the Granada Breeze studios in Manchester one Friday evening I heard someone calling my name as I was passing the security lodge for the *Coronation Street* studios. I turned to see the head of security for that area waving to me.

'I've a bit of a problem which I was hoping you could help me with,' he said. 'Some of the *Coronation Street* cast and back-room staff have encountered things that they just can't explain in the corridors close to the dressing rooms. My boss has asked whether you could do an investigation to find out what's going on, because whatever it is, it certainly isn't of this world!'

I agreed to return two days later on the Sunday when the area would be much quieter with fewer people around.

On the appointed day I met the head of security who took me into the building which houses the dressing rooms and led me to an area in the corridors where problems had been experienced. Cold spots had been noticed, light switches had been interfered with and door handles had been rattled. When the occupants of the dressing rooms had opened the door to investigate, there would be nobody there.

I quickly became aware that there was indeed spiritual energy and activity in the corridors. My first encounter was with a spirit individual whom I immediately recognized as Doris Speed. This lady had long played the character of Annie Walker, the landlady of the Rovers Return, a hostelry which she had ruled with a rod of iron.

Doris still considered that 'the Street' and its people were her concern and she was dismayed at the manner in which the bosses of the programme were treating her fellow actors and colleagues over an issue involving contracts. She was very upset that certain actors might be forced to leave *Coronation Street* and was determined to get her point across. 'They must listen!' she said. 'This must not happen! Do they want to lose *Coronation Street* altogether?'

Doris was still berating the powers that be when another very famous *Coronation Street* character who is now in the spirit world made her presence known. It was Annie Walker's arch-enemy Elsie Tanner! The lovely warm-hearted spirit of Pat Phoenix had decided that she too would like to voice her concern that certain actors had been singled out for particularly heavy treatment. Although she spent some time joking with me about making people jump when she rattled doorknobs, she was equally angry about the situation and wanted me to let everybody know that 'the old cast' were still looking out for their fellow actors, even if it was from another realm.

It was obvious that the two ladies were of the same mind, unlike their characters of years gone by. They were united in their wish that all the cast of *Coronation Street* should rally together, fight for their rights and stifle the problems which were prevailing at that time.

I moved a little further on and was taken completely by surprise when a spirit man made himself known to me. I could not see him but I knew that I was communicating with Peter Adamson, who had played the character of Len Fairclough. He still seemed to be a character of strong opinions. I will not repeat the content of his communication with me, but will say that just because a person has passed to the world of spirit it does not mean that their opinions and beliefs immediately change.

As I turned the corner of the corridor I made my final link with two lovely ladies. Pat Phoenix was one of them and this time she was joined by the *grande dame* of *Coronation Street*, Ena Sharples. I felt privileged to be sharing the atmosphere with the spirit of the great Violet Carson. Both women told me that for weeks they had been trying to draw attention to themselves by visiting the set and constantly turning lights on and off. Pat told me of a time when an electrical maintenance man had been attending to what he thought was a faulty light socket. He had been up a ladder completing his work when she had walked towards him. She had not realized that he was particularly sensitive to spirit and he had immediately detected a strange cold atmosphere approaching him. He had scurried down the ladder, but in doing so had stumbled and fallen to the floor. Fortunately he had not harmed himself, but she could not help laughing when she recalled him running off down the corridor. She asked me to pass on her apologies to him.

I shared in Pat's amusement and her impish sense of fun at the poor man. What a fright he must have had.

As I turned to leave the corridor, one of the dressing-room doors opened and there stood a good friend of mine, Bill Tarmey, who plays the character of Jack Duckworth. 'Derek! What're you doing here?' he asked. I told him that I had been asked to look around because of certain things which had happened. 'Yes,' he said, 'there have been quite a few funny goings-on just recently!'

I was very pleased to hear some weeks later that the problems had been sorted out and that all was peaceful and harmonious once more on *Coronation Street*.

THE BIRTH OF
MOST HAUNTED

It was a Sunday in March 2000 and I was scheduled to go to Manchester to film four studio sections of *Predictions with Derek Acorah*. On my arrival I was met by one of the producers, who told me that they had been contacted by the presenter Yvette Fielding, who, being a great fan of the programme, had asked whether she could come along to sit in the audience. I agreed immediately.

Later that day Yvette arrived and we were introduced. She told me that she was fascinated by my work and by the paranormal in general. She also told me that she had been experiencing some rather strange events in her home and wondered whether I could help her find out the cause. I agreed that I would visit her home at some point in the not too distant future to try to solve the problem.

A few weeks later Yvette, who at that time was presenting her own DIY programme for Granada Breeze, stood in for Becky Want, the regular *Predictions* presenter. It was on this occasion that she had a question for me. She and her husband Karl Beattie had come up with an idea for a programme. They wanted to make a pilot and asked me whether I would be willing to take part. Their idea was that they would take a group of people—a medium, a parapsychologist, camera and sound crew—around the country to alleged haunted locations to conduct investigations and attempt to catch paranormal activity on film. I, as the medium, would not be told prior to the investigation where I was going. Yvette would present the programme and the rest of the people involved would register their own experiences too.

It was an interesting concept. I would be doing exactly the same as I was for the *Predictions* investigations, but other people's experiences would also be filmed, with the parapsychologist providing the voice of reason. I agreed that I would take part.

The following Friday, after *Psychic Livetime*, Gwen and I joined Yvette and Karl in Pizza Express to discuss the matter further. This was the first time I had met Karl and although I felt that he was a deeply spiritual man, I also felt that he was rather sceptical of spirit communication and mediumship. Yvette was excitedly telling him of my success on the *Predictions* and *Psychic Livetime* programmes, but I knew that it would take a little more than hearsay to convince him that mediumship truly existed. The only way to provide proof was to give a couple of messages from the spirit world.

I opened myself up to Karl's vibrations and was immediately aware of a man who was standing beside him. 'You have a man with you,' I said, 'a grandfather, who tells me that his name is Frederick. He likes to be known as Frederick and wouldn't thank anybody for calling him Fred.'

Karl looked at me blankly.

I gave a little more information, but I could tell that I really wasn't making much of an impression. Oh dear!

Things weren't looking good. I had provided some proof, but Karl could not place the communicating spirit at all. Nevertheless he was very polite and told me that he had never met a medium before but would think about all the things I had to tell him. We continued our conversation about the forthcoming pilot programme and agreed on a date a couple of weeks hence for the filming.

On the appointed day Yvette and her brother Rick Fielding arrived at our home early in the morning. 'We've a long drive ahead,' Yvette told me. 'We're off to Sussex!'

Six weary hours later we arrived at the location. Karl walked up to me with his hand outstretched. 'Derek! Good to see you. Welcome to Michelham Priory. Oh, and by the way, that chap Frederick who you told me about last time we met—I didn't recognize the name at all at the time, but when I next saw my mother I asked her whether there was anybody in our family named Frederick. She told me that it was my grandfather. She also told me that he always insisted on being called Frederick and hated to have his name shortened to Fred. So you were right on everything you said, Derek. Now tell me—how d'you see this programme going? D'you think it'll be a success?'

I told him that of course he and Yvette would sell the programme, but it would not be without some initial difficulties. However, ultimately I saw the programme becoming a huge success. Since then *Most Haunted* has become the most watched paranormal programme on satellite television and has beaten all records. Long may its success continue! However, on that day in July it was just a prediction and we had an investigation to conduct.

We were taken to a barn which forms an annexe to Michelham Priory. I was introduced to the rest of the crew and together we sat around a long refectory table waiting for darkness to fall. I was talking to Jason, our trusty parapsychologist, when I caught sight of a movement up in the rafters. A small dark object swooped down and skimmed the top of our heads.

'What was that? It wasn't a bat because it was too big!' shouted Jason.

'No,' I said grimly, 'that was no bat. That was a dark spirit!'

I wondered what the night would hold as I mentally gathered spirit protection around me. I knew then that the investigations I would conduct with Yvette and the rest of the team would be far more terrifying than the *Predictions* investigations had ever been and would stretch my mediumship to its limits.

As we walked across the lawns towards Michelham Priory to commence the night's investigation, our shadows were cast against the mellow stonework of the old building and magnified tenfold as we passed in front of the security lights illuminating the priory. We reached the door, which made a gratifyingly eerie creak as I opened it. We entered a stark stone-walled room, sparsely furnished as it would have been when the priory was inhabited by the monks of long ago. In the corner of the room a dummy clad in brown robes presided over a ledger. The moon cast shadows around the stone pillars which supported the roof. It all looked so heart-stoppingly real you could almost imagine the dummy monk peering over his wire-rimmed spectacles and demanding to know our business within the priory.

Almost tiptoeing in the silence, we entered a corridor which led to the main part of the building. As we approached the stairway a door to the left of us swung open. Everyone jumped with surprise and Yvette gave a cry. Clutching hold of my arm, she sobbed, 'The door! It just opened on its own!'

Gingerly one of the crew stretched out an arm and tried to push the door. It didn't move an inch! This was no door swinging on well-oiled hinges.

'It wasn't a draught blowing open the door,' I said. 'It was opened by a spirit man and he's standing there now!'

Jason walked towards the door. As he got close the screech of his electromagnetic frequency meter echoed through the rooms and the temperature gauge dropped dramatically. Even he could not deny that there was evidence of spirit activity.

Sam told me to go to the kitchen. 'Don't worry, Derek,' he said. 'I'm here. You're perfectly safe.' I knew that Sam wouldn't tell me this for no reason, so the spirit who walked the empty kitchen must be a very strong spirit and I would need all my strength when I did at last meet him.

We crossed the stone-flagged kitchen, past the long-deserted kitchen range where once all manner of food would have been prepared. As I approached the doorway to a corridor leading from the kitchen I felt rather than saw the presence of a man—a large strong man who was not in the least pleased by our invasion of what he considered to be his property. As I stood in the doorway it felt as though this man was influencing me directly, as though I was growing both in height and girth. I struggled to speak, but all that came out was a strange strangled shout.

Jason approached once again, his EMF meter screeching loudly as he drew nearer to me. The temperature gauge, as he ran it around my body, registered a rapid drop in temperature.

'Sam, Sam!' I pleaded. 'Take this feeling away from me!'

Gradually, I felt the influence of the spirit entity draining away from me. As I slumped against the wall, I knew that I had met the dark spirit I had glimpsed so briefly in the barn earlier.

After I had taken a few moments to gather myself together once more, we left the kitchen, retreating away from the disruptive vibrations and into the dining room. As I passed the stairs I heard Sam telling me, 'There's a surprise up there, Derek! We'll show them later!'

Standing in the dining room next to the huge fireplace, I was confused. Sam had mentioned the staircase but I was being impressed by some unknown spirit with the information that there was another staircase—and that it was in this room!

'Sam,' I asked desperately, 'where is the staircase?'

'It's no longer here,' he told me. 'Many years ago it was removed, but people still see past memories ascending and descending in the place where it once was,' and he pointed to the fireplace beside which I was standing.

I was still puzzling over what Sam had said to me in the hallway. What would we show them? It was time to find out.

We mounted the stairs and as we did so Sam impressed me to start pushing at the wooden panels of the wall about halfway up the second flight. As I did so I felt one of the panels move. 'You've found the secret tunnel, Derek,' Yvette told me excitedly. Secret tunnel! So that was what Sam had been talking about.

'It's where Rosemary used to hide,' I heard Sam say. 'She used to bring her dolls. She put them in a box. They were her friends. She is afraid of the dark presence of the man you encountered in the kitchen.' This had to be looked into!

Ian went first, followed by Karl and me. But as Ian moved forward, he suddenly slipped and almost disappeared from view. Karl and I both lunged forward to catch him by the arms.

'Go no further, Derek,' Sam told me urgently. 'There is a spirit man here who isn't happy at all at the intrusion into his realms!'

With a superhuman effort, Karl and I managed to drag Ian back onto the floor of the secret passageway. 'We must leave this place,' I told everybody.

As we climbed out of the secret doorway a woman's laughter could be heard echoing through the old priory. We all looked at one another. There were only three women in the group—Yvette, Bev the director and Gwen—and they were all standing looking at one another on the stairs just outside the entrance to the secret passageway. A long-passed female spirit was obviously enjoying our brush with danger at the site of the old stairway.

It was time to move on, this time to the drawing room, once more with a guardian dummy dressed in monkish robes. Yvette gave a start. 'Somebody's just pinched me!' she exclaimed. It was the child Rosemary. We sat in a circle and prayed for her soul—that she would be guided to the light of the spirit realms and away from the man of whom she was so afraid. 'It is done!' said Sam.

Daylight began to break and the early-morning birds could be heard heralding the dawn. It was time to go, time to leave Michelham Priory to the spirits who walked the old building and looked upon it as their own.

As we turned to leave, one of the group glanced back into the drawing room. 'The chair!' he exclaimed. 'It's moved!' So it had—a chair which had been one of a set lining the walls had been moved about three feet towards the centre of the room. This was the last sign that the priory was indeed still the home of the many people who had once inhabited it in their earthly incarnations.

The End of an Era

On my return from Sussex I was due to appear on the Wednesday edition of *Psychic Livetime*. I arrived at the studios just before 5 p.m. and as I walked into the green room I noticed that there wasn't the usual light-hearted air about the place. People looked troubled.

'What's going on?' I asked Renée, one of the researchers for the programme.

'There's a rumour that Granada Breeze is going to cease all live programming so it'll be the end of *Psychic Livetime*, *Predictions* and all the other programmes we make here in Manchester,' she replied. 'That'll mean that we're all out of a job unless we can transfer over to mainline Granada, but there are so few jobs available there that we're all really worried.'

I have to admit that the closure of Granada Breeze had been the furthest thing from my mind. I hadn't dreamed that my work for the television company might cease to continue and Sam certainly hadn't stepped forward with any information. Now, however, I was desperate for answers!

Renée was looking at me expectantly, no doubt waiting for me to tell her not to worry, that all the jobs were safe and that we would continue. Unfortunately this was not to be the case. Sam was telling me that things were being wound down and that the live programming would cease shortly.

'They think the station will continue,' he told me, 'but it won't. By December Granada Breeze will be no more, but don't worry, Derek, your work for spirit will continue!'

I turned to Renée. How could I tell her that the job she loved was about to finish?

'I'm afraid that the outlook isn't good for Granada Breeze,' I told her. 'What I would advise you to do is start applying for positions with other television companies. Sam is telling me that you will be successful in an application.'

Some months later I bumped into Renée in Manchester and was delighted to hear that my prediction for her future had been correct. She had secured a position with another television company and was now an assistant producer.

The following Friday when I arrived at the studio, the atmosphere was worse. Some of the technical staff had been given notice and an article had appeared in a local newspaper confirming everybody's worst fears. The following Monday I received a telephone call to tell me that the *Psychic Livetime* show scheduled for 29 July would be the last one to go out live on air. From that date onward the station would continue, but instead of live programming, they would be airing shows brought in from America, together with repeats of the *Predictions* programme.

'It's a pity,' I told the programme controller at the time. 'People will realize that they've made a great mistake and the station won't be on air by next January!'

'Oh, I don't think so, Derek. I know that your programmes were highly popular, but these American shows should capture a large audience.'

'We'll see!' I replied.

Three years on I still speak regularly to that programme controller and time after time I have heard him say, 'If only we had kept the live programming, we might still be watching Granada Breeze to this day!'

Finally, the day that everybody dreaded arrived. I turned up at the studios as usual and everything followed the familiar pattern. The scheduled items went ahead as planned, the audience contacted the studio to speak to me on the usual live telephone link-up and Becky wound up the show as normal. The public had not been informed that this was to be the last ever *Psychic Livetime*.

As I drove home that evening, I reflected on all the good times I had experienced with Granada Breeze: the surprise fiftieth birthday party where the studio had been inundated by the self-styled 'Acorah Angels'—people who were regular visitors to my website and who had decided to form a fan club; the spoof 'dream' sequence when I had been dressed up in a pink sequinned top hat and tails and had stumbled my way through a script. I find it impossible to remember 'lines' and spent hours pre-recording the item, much to the frustration of the studio staff. I remembered when I had tested the patience of the technical staff to the limits with some of the mistakes I had made. I remembered all the people I had spoken to during my four years with the programme, either at the studio or live on air. I hoped that I had been able to help just a little with their problems and had given comfort and proof of life after physical death. I felt sad to know that it was all over, but I realized that my work with spirit would carry on. Sam had told me it would.

A NEW OPPORTUNITY

With the end of Granada Breeze in Manchester both Yvette and I were out of a job. I continued with my personal readings and of course I also had my theatre shows to look forward to. I was happy, though I missed the hurly-burly of the studio and the people I had worked with for the last four years.

Yvette and I spoke regularly on the telephone and in September she called me excitedly to tell me that they had completed the editing of the investigation at Michelham Priory. She invited Gwen and me to her home to meet up with the rest of the team and to view the programme, which she and Karl had decided to call *Haunting Truths*.

When we saw the programme, we were very optimistic. This visit also provided the ideal opportunity for me to try to find out who in the spirit world was causing the noises which were troubling Yvette and which we had discussed earlier in the year.

I managed to establish that the cause of the problems was a farmer's wife who was still bustling around what she considered still to be her home. She was completely harmless, but let me know that she was still keeping an eye on her domain.

Yvette's grandmother also communicated with me to let me know that she was looking after her grandchildren and was making sure that no harm would come to them.

In November I received a telephone call from a very excited Karl and Yvette. They had sold the programme to the satellite television company UK Living (now LIVINGtv), which had commissioned a 16-episode series of programmes which were to be named *Most Haunted*. Filming was to commence on 8 January 2001.

'You may wonder how "ghost hunting" can spread the word of spirit,' Sam chuckled. 'But you'll see, Derek! This programme will have people asking questions about the spirit world. Do your work to the best of your ability. Some people will question you and will not always be kind, but don't take any notice. You are working for spirit. This is the pathway you have chosen. Nobody promised you that it was going to be easy!'

How correct Sam's words turned out to be. Although most people are polite and kind to me, whether they are sceptical or not, certain people have been most offensive and nasty, even to the point of threatening my life. I have sometimes questioned the wisdom of carrying on, but as Sam said, 'Nobody said it was going to be easy!' And I know I am working for spirit.

THE POLTERGEIST
OF PENNY LANE

On a cold, bright February Sunday in 2000 I found myself driving to Liverpool and heading in the direction of Penny Lane, the street immortalized by the Beatles in their song of the same name. I had been invited to join Tom Slemen, local journalist and author of many books covering Liverpool's ghostly past, on an investigation of premises in Penny Lane where what seemed to be poltergeist activity had been experienced for many years.

I drove slowly along the lane and eventually arrived outside the shop where I was to meet Tom. As I did so the skies darkened and the wind began to blow skirmishes of browned leaves across the road from Sefton Park. I began to feel an oppression—a heaviness born of depression and unhappiness. I knew that the spirit person I was about to meet would be an unhappy soul. I also knew that he was aware of my imminent arrival and that he did not want me there.

I parked my car. The premises weren't quite what I had expected: a brightly lit property shop with day-glo stickers in the window. It looked light and airy and not the sort of place you would imagine harboured an unhappy spirit.

Tom was waiting for me together with Ronnie, the manager of the shop. Ronnie explained that he was quite sceptical about ghosts, but the events which had taken place in his shop had led him to contact Tom to try and find out exactly what was going on.

As I went through the door into the reception area I felt as though I was being drawn by some unseen force to the rear office of the shop. I knew as I walked towards that area that I would experience an inexplicable drop in temperature. I was not disappointed! This was a vortex—an area of the property where spirit entities would enter and exit our atmosphere.

At the back of the rear office a washroom had been constructed. When I opened the door to this washroom I came face to face with the man who haunts the shop in Penny Lane. This was his favourite place in the building.

In life he had been an arrogant soul, with the arrogance born of the insecurity of a misfit. He was the sort of person who blamed everybody but himself, though if he had truly taken stock he would have known that he wasn't helping himself by being like this. He was crafty and liked women, but was too shy to form normal relationships and would appease his lusting by slyly touching where he should not touch. When he passed over to spirit he enjoyed frightening and shocking people. It was this that had given the impression of poltergeist activity within the walls of this ordinary-looking suburban Liverpool store. I also knew that this man had had a reliance on alcohol. He had also had a depressive nature and had finally taken himself over to the world of spirit—he had committed suicide whilst in his fifties.

As I stood there in the small back office I knew that this unhappy soul had been regularly energized by the activities of more earthly beings. I gained the impression that three people had lived in the upstairs area of the property. They had amused themselves by using a ouija board. This had had the effect of allowing the man in spirit to feed off their energies. 'Oh yes!' he would say. 'You're giving me energy! Let me stay here!'

I felt that this sad spirit had been given the opportunity to pass into the light, but he did not want to go. He was afraid of the unknown, just as we in this earthly life are afraid. He preferred to stay in the corner of the room which was familiar to him, where he felt safe. Even though the property had changed beyond recognition from the days when he had lived there, he did not see those changes. To him the place remained as he had known it 50 years earlier.

As with any negative spirit, he would delight in causing problems with electrical appliances. I told Ronnie and Tom that I would like to bet that such problems had been experienced and that any efforts to heat the area had been ineffectual. Ronnie confirmed that no matter how hard they tried they could not heat the rear portion of the shop. Every heater placed in that area would malfunction.

I also mentioned that there was more than a likelihood that problems regarding water and pipes had been experienced. Ronnie confirmed that water damage from a bath overflow three years previously had still not dried out and the wall at the rear of the property was continually damp even though no water pipes were located in that area and it was an interior wall.

'I wouldn't be at all surprised if, after we have gone, some problems with boxes and papers are experienced,' I told Ronnie. Later that day whilst on my way home I received a telephone call informing me that boxes of paper had indeed been knocked over and spread around the office.

Back in the office, my talking about his secrets had obviously angered the spirit man and he tried to move closer to me, causing me to cough and splutter as my chest tightened.

'You know, Derek, I'm amazed,' Tom said. 'I could swear that I've just seen a face over your right shoulder and it wasn't a very nice-looking face at all!'

'You're right, Tom. He's just tried to close in on me in an attempt to stop me talking about him.'

I mentally attuned myself with Sam. 'Take him away,' I whispered softly.

The temperature in the room started to rise as I resisted the efforts of this horrible spirit to draw close to me. Then I was impressed by the name 'Jim'. 'In fact there are two Jims,' I said, 'but they're not associated with the chap we've just been dealing with!'

'That's right, Derek! The shop was owned by a person called Jim and he had a son of the same name. And by the way, there was a suicide here!' Tom told me.

'And there's a lady coming in here too,' I went on, 'although she's more associated with the upstairs. She's a young lady with long flowing hair.'

Tom was there again to confirm that a lady had been seen in the window of the upstairs room on numerous occasions. She was always seen brushing her long hair.

We moved towards the front part of the shop. As we did so I felt a coolness follow us and there was the all-pervading stench of stale drink. As we stood in the middle of the front office I heard a crash behind me.

'The tripod!' Tom shouted. 'I saw it twist and turn before it fell!'

'Get away!' I shouted out into the ether. 'Leave this place!'

It was time for us to leave, but as I turned and looked in Tom's direction I was surprised to see yet another spirit man building up beside him. I knew that this man had nothing whatsoever to do with the shop and that in fact he belonged to Tom.

'Your father's here,' I told him. 'He was a big man, quite bald, strong and kind-hearted. He was a quiet person who thought things out before speaking. He sends all the love in the world to you. He talks of a lady who has leg problems and sends great love to her too.'

'Yes, that's my dad,' said Tom quietly. 'He passed over about six months ago and my mum is the person with the leg problems.'

'There's a birthday celebration soon. Send some flowers to your sister.'

'I will,' Tom laughed, 'but why is he here?'

I told him that his father had just come along because he was interested in what Tom was doing. 'And by the way, he says, "Me ticker's OK now!"'

'That's right,' Tom confirmed. 'That's what got him in the end!'

Tom was pleased that I had been able to prove to him that his father still lived on in the spirit world and I was touched by his effusive thanks.

'Just make sure that you remember to send those flowers!' I joked with him.

'Oh, I will,' he said.

THE PYRAMID TOMB

It was early afternoon. 'If you don't mind, Derek, I'd like you to visit another haunted site with me before it gets dark,' Tom said. 'Would you be willing to do that? It's only about 15-minutes' drive away from here.'

I wondered what Tom had up his sleeve now. We climbed into our cars and I followed Tom as he headed off in the direction of Liverpool city centre. As we passed the shadows of the Anglican cathedral, we turned right into Rodney Street, the Harley Street of Liverpool, where doctors and surgeons have their consulting rooms. Although I had travelled down this street on numerous occasions and had been vaguely aware of a derelict church, I hadn't noticed the graveyard next to that church. I was certainly unaware of the peculiar pyramid-shaped tomb to which Tom pointed as we alighted from our vehicles.

'That's it, Derek. I'd like you to tell me what impressions you're getting from the tomb over there.'

The graveyard has a six-foot, iron-railing fence along the front of it on Rodney Street. A huge brick wall, at least 15 or 16 feet high, runs along its perimeter on the small side street. As I was standing peering through the railings looking at the tomb I was amazed to see two men in spirit, both very tall and very thin, materialize at the doorway set at the front of the pyramid. They wore blue and silver headbands and had belted aprons of the same colour. One of them appeared to be holding what looked like a sceptre. I had the impression that they were the guardians of secret knowledge, of a type of masonic secrecy which men would involve themselves in in the past and still do to this very day. One of the men appeared to beckon towards me. I knew that somehow I had to get nearer to the tomb.

I scanned along the railings looking for a break where it might have been possible for us to squeeze through, but there wasn't one. I looked towards the wall, hoping that there might be a gap, but no, just like the fence, it was solid and far too high for us to jump over. As I looked along its length I noticed in the distant corner a huge solid wooden gate. Would it be possible to squeeze through?

We walked towards the gate but as we approached it I could see that it was soundly padlocked. There was no possibility of squeezing in. The only solution was to scale the wall. The hinges of the gates afforded a toehold, but it was a long way up for a 50-year-old man and a very long drop down on the other side. 'Oh well! Here go the knees again!' I thought to myself.

After a great deal of scrambling and the expected knee-shuddering drop down onto the other side of the wall, we finally managed to gain entry into the graveyard. As I approached the pyramid tomb my attention was diverted to a gravestone which stood quite close to it. A very slim spirit lady stood nearby. She was quite tall with light brown hair. She had been a true lady in her earthly form—a loving and knowledgeable woman. I knew that she had met up with her two sons who had passed to spirit as small children. I had the definite impression that her name was Janet and that she was in some way connected to the man whose physical remains were contained in the pyramid tomb. She said nothing, merely smiled a serene smile and nodded at me as I passed by.

As I drew closer to the pyramid I became ever more certain that this place contained some form of knowledge. I was also aware that great negativity had played a part in the life of the occupant when here on Earth. The name 'James' was echoing through my mind, followed a moment or two later by another name: 'MacKenzie'. Were those two names connected with the pyramid?

I knew that deaths had taken place—deaths which should have been registered, but were not. Somebody had changed the records to cover up for a number of wrong-doings. I knew that many, many souls had been lost and the manner of their passing and the subsequent disappearance of their earthly remains were somehow tied up with the man whose physical body now occupied the Rodney Street pyramid. I had a mental image of a long stone tablet, about five feet or more long, masonic symbols and two keys. The words 'The Administrator of Light' kept repeating themselves in my head.

By now it was growing quite dark. Tom and I found that we were stumbling on the uneven surface of the deserted graveyard. Clipped lawns were certainly not the order of the day here! We were beginning to find that the many broken headstones strewn around were becoming increasingly hazardous. 'We'd better go, Derek,' said Tom. 'We've still got to get back over that gate!'

I was frustrated that I hadn't been able to come up with any definite answers, but Tom seemed happy with the information that I had given him. After a supreme effort we managed to get back over the gate. Tom thanked me and told me that what I had said was of great help to his investigations regarding the pyramid tomb. Then he told me that it was his aim to secure permission to X-ray the tomb to finally lay to rest the story of James MacKenzie's pact with the Devil!

Tom was kind enough to write an account in a local newspaper the following week:

I rarely use psychics or mediums during my investigations into hauntings and paranormal phenomena, frankly because I have never been impressed with people who profess to be in communication with the dead but can never produce a surname, just a 'John' or a 'Mary'.

Many mediums I have encountered over the years have used little more than blatant hypnotic suggestion on gullible people genuinely seeking knowledge about loved ones who have passed over to the other side.

However last week I decided to give a psychic named Derek Acorah a try. He was literally a random choice and when I asked if I could put him to the test by taking him to several well-researched haunted dwellings with a view to contacting a supernatural entity, Derek was very enthusiastic about the proposal.

The rendezvous was 44 Penny Lane, the abode of a particularly durable poltergeist and also the premises of a student accommodation agency.

I had made prior arrangements with the manager to open the shop on Sunday and as soon as Derek arrived on the premises he zeroed straight in on the small backroom of what had been an epicentre of terrifying poltergeist activity since 1930.

This room is now used as the shop staff room. What followed next was both sensational and unexpected.

Derek gave me the name of the man who committed suicide at number 44 way back in the 1940s. The living descendants of the unfortunate man have asked me to refrain from giving his name so I have to comply with their wishes, but Derek not only revealed the man's name to me, he also told me the exact tragic circumstances of the man's suicide.

As Derek was standing in the room a misty-looking form appeared in front of me and a witness and almost solidified into what appeared to be a contorted distressed face. Derek calmly told me that this was a manifestation of the suicide which had taken the man's life and the medium then claimed that his spirit guide 'Sam' was present overseeing things.

Seconds later the eerie-looking face dissolved like a vapour and Derek seemed very pale and drained.

When he had recovered back in the shop he told me there were more earthbound entities present from different time periods.

He also warned me that the embittered suicide entity would become hostile because it had been disturbed and identified. Less than ten minutes after Derek had left the room to visit another haunted site with me there was a loud nerve-shattering clatter in the staffroom and when the manager nervously went to investigate he found a box of A4 paper had scattered its contents under a table.

Derek's unearthly talents were later put to the test once more in Rodney Street where we scaled the 18-foot wall of a cemetery to take a look at the pyramidal tomb of James MacKenzie, a Victorian whose spinechilling shade has been seen by dozens of witnesses over the years.

The psychic impressions Derek received in the proximity of this tomb were not only uncannily accurate, they also answered many seemingly unsolvable puzzles that had confounded me for years.

BEREAVEMENT

And now life in its term has evolved death, for not nature only, but man's being has its seasons—its sequence of spring, summer, autumn and winter. If someone is tired and has gone to lie down we do not pursue him with shouting and bawling. She whom I have lost has lain down to sleep for a while in the great inner room—to break in upon her rest with the noise of lamentation would be but to show that I knew nothing of nature's sovereign law. That is why I cease to mourn.

—*A Chinese Taoist's View of Death*

The most difficult part of our lives here on this earthly plane is when the time comes for us to part physical company with people who have meant so much to us. At the time of their passing into the world of spirit many of us are left feeling as though we are unable to come to terms with the fact that our loved ones have moved on.

In fact they may have moved on physically, but they have not gone away from us, they have merely progressed into another realm—the spirit realm. They have shed their earthly garb but still remain with us, unseen to the physical eye. They continue to care for us and monitor our daily lives, but just as they were not constantly with us in life, so they are not constantly with us after their passing to the world of spirit. They will come to protect us at stresssful times of our lives and may inspire us with solutions when problems arise. The one thing that they never do is abandon us.

On 26 June 2000 my wife Gwen's mother Joan passed on to the spirit world. We loved her dearly and her physical presence was sorely missed by both of us. She was a second mother to me and we used to share many fun times together. Although she was 80 years of age and burdened by many physical difficulties, she never lost her sense of humour nor her belief that when her time came to be reunited with Gwen's father in the spirit world we would be able to continue the conversations, the jokes and the joyous banter that we had when she was here with us.

At the time of Joan's passing we received the following verse written by Henry Scott Holland, which I think sums up all that we should remember when we lose a loved one to spirit. I would like to share it with you:

DEATH IS NOTHING AT ALL

Death is nothing at all
I have only slipped away into the next room;
I am I and you are you—
Whatever we were to each other,
That we still are.
Call me by my old familiar name;
Speak to me in the easy way
Which you always used,
Put no difference in your tone,
Wear no forced air of solemnity or sorrow,
Laugh as we always laughed
At the little jokes we enjoyed together.
Let my name be ever the household word
That it always was.
Let it be spoken with effect
Without the trace of a shadow on it.
Life means all that it ever meant.
It is the same as it ever was.
There is unbroken continuity.
Why should I be out of mind
Because I am out of sight.
I am waiting for you, for an interval,
Somewhere very near, just around the corner.
All is well!

If you have lost someone who is very dear to you to the world of spirit, I hope that this verse will bring the same comfort and reassurance that it gave to Gwen and her family.

STILL CARING

Joan had a tremendous sense of humour and was always joking with me about my football playing. 'You should have played rugby,' she used to tell me. 'Now *that's* a man's game!' She and Gwen's father had been brought up in Widnes and were ardent supporters of the local team, whose colours happened to be black and white. Just before Joan's passing I had been considering purchasing a new car and had mentioned that I would like a red one. Joan used to jokingly tut and raise her eyes. Two weeks after she had passed to spirit I bought my new vehicle. What colour was it? It was black with a white vinyl top! Try as I might, I couldn't find a red vehicle which was suitable. As I drove away I could hear a chuckle in my ear. It was Joan. 'Now that *is* a nice colour!' she said.

More proof of Joan's loving care and protection occurred some weeks later. Gwen and I had planned to travel to a *Predictions* location using Gwen's car. We had loaded the vehicle up with overnight bags and our two dogs, who were going to stay with Gwen's daughter Jayne whilst we were away overnight.

We set off but got no further than the traffic lights at the end of the road when the engine died. Try as we might, the engine just would not fire. We managed to park the vehicle up and trudged back to the house with the dogs in tow to arrange for the local garage to collect and repair the car.

When we arrived back late the following day we received surprising news. The garage could find nothing at all wrong with the engine but had found a dangerous mechanical condition with the rear axle. Had we used the car to travel on the motorway we would most certainly have been involved in a serious accident and could quite easily have been killed. As the manager of the garage regaled me with this information I had a fleeting vision of Joan's face smiling at me. I knew that she had been watching out for us and had caused the engine to fail in order to save us from what could have been a disaster.

Later that year, on 16 November, my own dear father Fred passed to the world of spirit after finally succumbing to that horrible disease, cancer, which he had successfully fought and overcome 15 years earlier. To the end of his physical life he retained his sense of humour and helped us—my mother and his children—to come to terms with the fact that he would be leaving us to join his other family in the world of spirit.

In his last days with us he was often visited by members of his family from the spirit world—his mother who had passed to spirit when he was just 11, his father, his sisters and friends. He was collected by his own father James, his mother Esther and his two sisters, Mary and Julia.

It was some weeks after his passing that I saw him for the first time. As I was sitting in my home meditating I saw Dad in the distance. He raised his arm to me in salute. 'Don't worry, son,' he told me. 'I'll be back!'

My father was a wonderful man who always had a kind word for everyone and who enjoyed meeting and greeting people on a daily basis. He was always proud of his children and would literally glow whilst talking about us. He spent the major part of his working life at sea in the Merchant Navy. He had joined at the age of 14 as a galley boy. He was proud that he eventually became head chef and indeed he spent several years in America in that capacity, but the love of the sea always drew him back. His spirit was now free to sail the seven seas and to visit the faraway lands he loved to talk to us about.

At home he was a man of simple tastes who enjoyed his family life and his garden, especially his garden pond, in which he kept his Koi carp. In fact it was his enthusiasm which encouraged me to take up fish keeping as a hobby myself. Nowadays we often share a few words whilst I carry out the daily tasks of looking after my own Koi. Dad is always there with a bit of advice.

PASSING OVER

The passing to spirit of Gwen's parents and my own father came at a time in their lives when, due to age and illness, it did not come as a huge shock to anybody when they finally made that ultimate journey. Of course at any age it is a most distressing and difficult thing to deal with, and the feelings of loss, of not being able to visit or talk on the telephone, are devastating. The knowledge is there, however, that a natural progression has been made from this life to the next and all is as it should be.

In contrast, people whose loved ones have taken themselves over to the higher side of life often wonder whether these sad and disturbed souls will enter the spirit world in exactly the same way. The answer to this is most definitely yes. Upon passing from this physical world, everybody progresses to the world of spirit. It does not matter who that person is, what they have done or how their passing came about.

Some years ago I had to deal with a situation which involved a case of suicide. It was the end of a very busy day in my consulting rooms in Victoria Street, Liverpool, and I was about to commence my last sitting. It was for a lady in her middle thirties who introduced herself as Pamela.

As I opened myself up to Pamela's vibrations I was horrified at the pictures I was viewing. I saw a man with three children and I could sense a great deal of unhappiness and despair, feelings of giving in and not wanting to go on. Pamela was looking at me expectantly. Her vibrations were light and calm and did not seem to fit in at all with the pictures which were unfolding.

I proceeded with her sitting. I communicated with a number of her loved ones who had passed to spirit and gave her proof of their survival. I spoke of her career and what she could expect to happen over the next few months. But all the time I was desperately wondering how I could convey to her the tragic events which were to take place in her life. Finally, I could put it off no longer, but I couched my words in the broadest of terms. I told her that if a person chooses to take their own life, they too go on to the world of spirit in exactly the same way as anybody who passes through natural causes. I continued by telling her that even if a person has their life taken away from them suddenly, either at the hands of another or through an accident, the system remains the same:

they go on to live in the heavenly state. Our loved ones never go away; they remain close to us.

Pamela looked perplexed. She did not understand what I was telling her, but I had done my best. I could not tell her bluntly that in approximately 18 months' time her husband would put her three children into a car and proceed to send all four of them over to the world of spirit. No medium would bluntly state to a querent, 'Look, your marriage is going to fall apart and as a result your husband's going to commit suicide and take your children with him.' It just would not happen with responsible mediumship. You read horror stories about people receiving messages from 'psychics' with very fertile imaginations, but these horror stories are rarely borne out (thank goodness), though it can be hugely upsetting for the poor recipient.

Pamela stood up. 'Well, Derek,' she said, 'thank you for the reading. I enjoyed it very much, but I'm afraid that towards the end you must have got your wires crossed. The messages that you gave me don't apply to me at all.'

I bowed my head. We shook hands and Pamela left my office.

It was almost two years to the day that I received a letter from Pamela:

I'd like firstly to apologize to you, Derek. Two years ago I came to see you in your office in Liverpool. Although the majority of the reading you gave me was absolutely spot on, I recall that at the end of the reading you gave me some information which I just could not understand. I told you that you were talking rubbish. It was approximately 18 months later, immediately after my husband had committed suicide by connecting a pipe to the car's exhaust, that I realized what you were trying to tell me. The most tragic part of this is that he took my three darling children with him. If it had not been for you, Derek, I doubt whether I would be here today, as I would have brought my own life to an end. I can only thank you for your words and apologize for not understanding. You are a very special man. Long may your work continue.

I was saddened by Pamela's letter, but was grateful that she had at least gained some comfort from my words. I knew that her husband would have entered the world of spirit and after a period of recuperation would have gently been guided through a learning process. Their children would have passed into the higher realms and would reside there until their spirits chose to reincarnate into this physical world once more.

What people do not realize when tragedy occurs is that those spirits chose to undergo that experience. Before incarnation into this physical life a spirit is given the opportunity to choose to experience all facets of physical life. We all have to undergo lessons in order to earn soul growth. Through many lifetimes we learn valuable lessons and have the possibility of evolving to a plane where incarnation into a physical life is no longer necessary.

It is my belief that before we incarnate into this life, we choose a pathway. That pathway may meander a little from its course, but ultimately we fulfil all our destinies one way or another to achieve soul growth. Nobody can interfere with that. In this case, for example, if I had told Pamela bluntly of the outcome of her decision to divorce her husband, she may not have done so, for the sake of both him and their children, but then I would have been directly interfering with a person's free will and pathway in life. Spiritual law just doesn't allow this.

REGRETS

When someone passes to spirit, people sometimes worry that they have crossed swords with them and they have not had the opportunity to say sorry. They worry that the person now residing in the world of spirit will not know how much they regret that they did not part on good terms. The following story emphasizes the fact that the people in spirit do not hold grudges.

I was at my home one evening when the telephone rang. I answered, to hear a man's voice saying, 'I'm desperate for help and guidance. Would it be possible for me to see you tomorrow?'

I had a full book of appointments for the following day, but such was the desperation in the man's voice that I agreed to see him in my lunch hour.

The next morning as I travelled to my office I began to feel very agitated. This is most unusual for me. I then began to feel as though I was choking and had the impression of falling into a darkened atmosphere. I became aware of a lady's spirit trying very hard to communicate with me. I pulled the car over to a safe spot at the curb. The spirit lady informed me that 'John' who was coming to see me at 1 p.m.

was her deranged husband. She was very bitter about him. Little did I know at that point the full story.

One o'clock arrived and John walked into my office. 'Thank you for seeing me so quickly,' he said. I replied that I knew now that he was meant to see me. At that, he looked at me rather strangely, but we commenced the reading. The spirit lady who had made her presence known to me during my drive into work quickly appeared. She stood silently as I spoke to her husband. I told him that there appeared to be a very strong negative influence around him and his life at that time.

He nodded in agreement. 'Can you tell me any more about this, Derek?' he asked.

I told him that I could see a male friend who was not a sensitive person who seemed to have some sort of hold over him. 'I feel that you have a deep regret over something which happened only six months ago concerning a lady.' John agreed. 'I can see that you had been a very happily married family man, then from out of the blue, your feelings changed. I feel that if you could turn back the clock you would most certainly do so.' At this point John's wife impressed me with the feelings that she would like her husband to know that she was present in the office. 'John, I must tell you that whilst I am conducting this reading, there has been the spirit of a lady here with us. She has red hair cut very short, she has blue eyes and on her arms she would have had some minor psoriasis. She tells me that her name is Maggie.'

Tears flowed from John's eyes. 'Please continue, Derek,' he said. 'Do you want to know who the lady is?'

'No,' I told him, 'the lady's telling me that she is your wife. She says that had a certain man not come into your life, all would have been well and happy. She tells me that she took an overdose of tablets because she could not bear it that you were having a relationship behind her back, especially not with a man!'

John put his head in his hands. He was sobbing uncontrollably. 'I know that Maggie's here with us,' he said. 'Nobody could know all those facts about me. God forgive me. Maggie, please, please forgive me.'

At this point Maggie said to me that she was becoming more sympathetic towards her husband because of his obvious sorrow. She told me she had noticed since her passing that John had deep regrets because his relationship with the man had turned somewhat sour. He had been thinking just recently about what he had entered into and for the first time he had been searching his soul. She had been trying to influence him recently to seek out the services of a medium in order that she could communicate with him. She did not want him living an unhappy life.

'Typical Maggie!' John said. 'Always trying to give me advice! I feel like a murderer. Please forgive me, Maggie. I should have been a better husband. I'm terribly sorry.'

Maggie herself was only just holding back her own tears after listening to her husband opening up his heart. 'Tell him I forgive him,' she said. 'Tell him that I'm not free of blame either. Looking back, I could have found a better solution than taking my own life. I could have divorced him and tried to get on with my life, but I allowed a great depression to envelop me.'

John listened intently to this.

Another lady in spirit then entered. She announced herself as Catherine, John's mother. John smiled and told me that she had passed to spirit whilst he had been married. Catherine had liked Maggie and now told me she still spent time with her in the spirit realms. She passed on the message that all was well and that John would later meet a young lady who would make him very happy. Maggie was overjoyed that her husband would at last find serenity and peace.

ANIMALS AND ANGELS

'Do animals have souls and do they pass on into the spirit world?' is a question which I am frequently asked. Of course they do. They are God's creatures, just as we are. At the end of their physical lives here on Earth they pass into the world of spirit to await the time when we will be reunited with them. I am looking forward to the day when I meet up once more with my beautiful German shepherd Cara.

It was when the time was drawing near for Cara to pass into the world of spirit that I had an encounter with one of the highly evolved celestial beings which are known to us as angels. They are always around us, but few people ever experience their presence.

It was a summer afternoon and I was sitting by the fish-pond in my garden. I had lost my dear father, Fred, to the world of spirit the previous November, and now my beloved dog was very old and I knew that soon she would be leaving me too. I was feeling very sad as I sat there staring into the water. I had lost one dear friend and was about to lose another. People may not understand that mediums still experience the feelings of grief and loss when a beloved person or pet passes from our physical world and on to the world of spirit. We are human and we suffer human emotions. We feel as other people feel. The fact that we know of the world beyond and spend our lives communicating with that world does not take away the fact that we grieve for the physical presence of someone or something that we love.

As I sat on that garden bench I suddenly heard a gentle rustling noise to my right and over my head. A feeling of warmth and peace seemed to spread over me, encompassing my whole body. I opened my eyes and looked up. Above me was the most magnificent being. All I could do was look and stare in wonderment. No words were spoken—there was no need. The feelings were sufficient.

My angel placed his ethereal arm around my shoulders and chest. I knew that he was giving me total love and protection. I was overcome with feelings of joy, compassion and beauty. I could not see my garden. I was enveloped in a pure white light which dazzled my eyes. I felt tears of joy running down my face as I bathed in the beauty and peace which surrounded me.

The light evaporated almost as a morning mist disappears in sunshine and I was left sitting on the garden bench, once more alone. I looked down to the floor. Lying there was a solitary white feather, its fronds moving gently in the light summer breeze. I felt warmth and happiness surrounding me. My sadness was gone.

My father's face appeared briefly before me. He looked so young and happy. He winked as he whispered to me, 'Don't worry, son, I'll look after her for you.' He was reaffirming to me that in a very short time when Cara's time came to pass to the world of spirit he would be there waiting for her.

Three short weeks later I had to make the decision which I had long dreaded. Cara had become quite ill and could not walk. Her breathing had become difficult. She had achieved the grand old age of 17 years, which for a German shepherd was something of a phenomenon.

On that fateful morning as she lay on her bed we both knew that the time had come for us to part. I reluctantly picked up the telephone and spoke to the vet, who came out to the house immediately. As Cara's spirit departed from her physical body I knew that she was going on to a heavenly state and that she would be met by my father.

Since that sad day I have seen Cara around our home on many occasions. She returns to sit in her favourite places and occasionally I will hear her bark. I have seen her clairvoyantly as she bounds joyously across the fields, young once more and not burdened by the ravages of age, and I know that she is being cared for by my father until we can be reunited.

CONNECTIONS

*W*alking along the Santa Monica, California pier was almost like walking along any UK coastal resort pier. There were fairground rides and a Ferris wheel, but ahead of me people were fishing into the deep waters of the Pacific Ocean and pelicans were dipping in their search for dinner. Pacific Pallisades, home to many famous Hollywood stars, could be seen in the distance to my right and to the left lay a band of almost yellow smog—all that could be seen of the great city of Los Angeles.

It was my first morning in Santa Monica. It was October 2001 and I had left the cold and damp of England's autumn behind as I had been invited to California to make a programme, *Connections with Derek Acorah*. The programme would be in two parts—one would involve me walking around the streets of Santa Monica offering readings for people as they went about their Saturday-morning shopping; the other would be a demonstration of mediumship before a live audience.

It was ironical that the first people I would meet would be a lovely couple from Birmingham. 'Derek Acorah! What are you doing here? We watch you every week on *Predictions* and *Psychic Livetime!*'

It was arranged that as I walked along I would indicate to the producer of the programme which people I could see a spirit presence with. The producer would then approach those people and ask if they would like a psychic from England to do a reading for them. Contrary to what was expected, this request was not initially well received and people refused, hastily moving away whilst looking back warily over their shoulders. Who was this oddball Englishman tramping around saying he could speak to dead people?

Eventually, when we had almost given up hope of anybody agreeing to a reading from me, a kind lady took pity and warily agreed that I could speak to her. Thank goodness! I was beginning to feel like an alien!

I was able to tell the lady that her mother and father were with her and that her father had been a big heavy-set man and had a strong connection with the police force. As I was relating these details to her, my voice became croaky and I was almost whispering.

'My God!' she exclaimed. 'You sound just like my father before he passed away with throat cancer, and he was in the L.A. Police Department too!'

'It's his influence that's making me speak this way,' I explained to her. 'He's talking to me about a lady who's with him. This lady passed to the spirit world with stomach cancer. They both send their love to you and are telling you, "Good luck with the health farm."'

'That has completely freaked me out!' came the response. 'My mother did pass with cancer of the stomach and I am in the health farm business! Thank you so much! You've helped me to believe. I was always sceptical before, but now I know that Mom and Dad are OK!'

It is amazing what a couple of cameras around a group of people can do. It wasn't long before people were stopping us wanting to know about their loved ones or what life had in store for them. I was able to pass on many messages of comfort and reassurance. A young lady was told by her mother Mary that the house move she'd been so desperately awaiting was about to happen, that she'd be rid of the disruptive neighbours who were making her life a misery. A woman in spirit called Betty spoke to her daughter, sending love but ticking her off gently for taking time away from work and gossiping unkindly about a friend. A young man from Cleveland was given hope for the future when he was told that divorce was not looming but that he and his wife would be back together again very soon—his father Scott who had passed to spirit as a result of a traffic accident was telling me so. Freda from Maine was tearfully grateful when her mother Jessie came through to talk to her and tell her that she should not blame herself because she hadn't been with her at the end.

I think my favourites, though, were the two ladies who were ecstatic to receive messages from their mother and their father, Jim. Their brother-in-law, also in spirit and also named Jim, also popped in to say hello. 'Hello, Jim!' they both shouted out whilst waving gaily in a direction somewhere over my left shoulder. I told them that their mother and father had been to visit their brother Ted in Florida and other details of their life, with which they readily agreed. As I was finishing speaking to them I asked if the reading had been alright for them. 'Oh yes, young man—we enjoyed it very much! It was wonderful!'

And as an aside, as they were signing the release forms, they added with a glint in their eyes, 'If there's anything sneaky going on here, our brother in Florida's a lawyer!'

I laughed. 'There's nothing sneaky going on, ladies. It's just Sam and I doing what we love to do best.'

ORANGE COUNTY

The second part of the programme involved travelling to Orange County to give readings to a live studio audience. Before meeting my audience I was given time to take a solitary walk around the grounds and gardens of the studio.

Although winter was fast approaching in the UK, here the sun beat down strongly and glinted off the droplets of water thrown up by the central fountain of a pond. It was such a peaceful place, beautifully landscaped with bougainvillaea and drooping willows.

Through the branches of the trees I suddenly noticed what looked like a tall pillar of concrete. Even more strangely, the pillar was covered in what looked suspiciously like graffiti. 'How awful that somebody has come in and spoiled such a beautiful garden,' I thought to myself.

As I wandered closer I could see that what I had thought from a distance was a pillar was in fact a huge slab of concrete which was reinforced throughout by long rusted iron rods. The once smooth surface was pitted and broken in places and the whole thing was covered in crude and garishly coloured symbols of peace, names and other words I did not understand, as they were written in a foreign language. I leaned forward and placed the flat of my hand on the surface, only to hastily withdraw it. I could feel the horrors of war! I could sense the hurt and desperation of people trying to escape. I experienced feelings of determination born of no choices.

I was touching a piece of the Berlin Wall which had been transported over to California and placed in this tranquil garden to remind the people of America of the hardships suffered in other parts of the world. How strange that I should be here, standing next to a piece of history, when not three weeks before, New York had been devastated by the events of September 11th.

It was time for me to leave the garden and enter the studio to prepare myself for meeting my audience. I started with a brief reading for a lady in the front row who was flanked by her two young daughters. 'Your grandmother's love surrounds the two girls,' I told her. 'She's talking about Italy. She says, "Mention Italy!" She's talking about Tony and says she likes him. She gives me the name "Barbara".'

The lady nodded. 'I'm Barbara and Tony is my boyfriend. He's from Italy. We hope to be married one day, so I'm really pleased that Grandma likes him.'

'I have a young woman here with me now,' I continued. 'She lost a lot of weight and was glad to let go at the end. She says to tell you that it's Laura and her friendship is still as strong as ever. She's also telling me that one of the girls has to go to the dentist soon. Oh, and in your home, there's been recent evidence of water-flow problems. You must get a plumber in.'

Barbara smiled through her tears. Laura was her best friend who had passed some two years earlier. 'It's just like Laura to worry about the girls,' she said. 'Becky does have a cavity in her tooth and I will get a plumber in, as I have been having a problem with water pipes in the laundry.'

A lady in spirit was building up beside me. 'I'm Elizabeth,' she told me. I knew that she was not connected with Barbara but that I had moved on to another audience member. Elizabeth then walked over and stood behind a gentleman in the audience. She placed her hand on his shoulder and told me, 'He's mine!'

'I'd like to come to you, sir, if you'll agree?' I asked. The gentleman nodded. 'I have a lady who's standing next to you. Her name is Elizabeth and she tells me that you are hers. She would have been about 5′6″ in height and of medium build. She wore her hair drawn back and is very motherly of nature. She had stomach problems before she passed to the world of spirit. She shows a huge amount of love and tenderness towards you and sends you a spiritual kiss.'

Tears streamed down the man's face. 'That's my mom,' he said quietly.

'Elizabeth is talking to me about an invitation you've received recently to go to the mountains. She tells me that you should accept this invitation, as it will do you good to get away.'

The man agreed that his boss had just bought a cabin in the mountains and he had indeed been asked to spend some time there on holiday. 'If Mom thinks it's a good idea, I'll definitely accept and take the family up there,' he laughed. 'She always gave good sound advice!'

'Who is Steve?' I asked.

'That's my boss,' came the reply.

'Elizabeth's now talking to me about a gentleman who has a lung condition—she mentions asbestosis. She tells me that he must look after himself—and that project to do with the home which you've been talking about, you must get on with it, but don't let Dad get involved as it'll be too much for him. She talks about Ted.'

'That's me,' the man replied. 'I'm Ted and so is my father. He's another Ted. There is something I've been planning to do with the house and Dad wants to help but because his chest has been affected by asbestos, I'll just let him assist in an advisory capacity!'

'Elizabeth tells me that you take after your father—he was good with his hands. She tells me that you can't go wrong if you follow his inspiration.'

Ted laughingly agreed and told me that his father had been a master carpenter. He had enjoyed his work so much that he had continued it on as a hobby from his workshop at home.

Elizabeth was satisfied that I had passed her messages on to her beloved son and that he was assured that she was still looking after him and his father even though she was no longer with them in the physical world. I knew that Ted was comforted by the knowledge that his mother was still around him guiding and inspiring him on his life's pathway.

My next message was for a lady at the back of the audience. 'I have a lady in spirit who was vivacious and very good-looking when she was young. She loves you dearly and misses you. She knows that you love her. She gives me the name Ellie and tells me that she is with her sister Lucy who passed to spirit with a cancerous condition though she would not have complained at all. She tells me that you are her daughter Donna! She wants to uplift your emotions and tell you that there is a lot of love ahead for you.'

The audience member I was talking to looked stunned. 'Yes, I'm Donna,' she said. 'I didn't believe that this was possible. I came here today totally sceptical and was looking forward to going away to tell my friends that mediums were rubbish!' She looked embarrassed as she added, 'But now I know, of course, that you're not rubbish at all.'

I continued, 'A man is coming close to me. He was full of face but had lost quite a lot of hair prior to his passing. He is smiling away at you and telling me that he is your grandfather. He's talking about electrical appliances and tells me that something needs to be changed.'

Donna nodded her agreement.

'I'm now being told that you have sought the assistance of a lawyer. I'm being taken into the lawyer's office and

I'm told that you want things sorted out. It will be, because you deserve it. Everything will be sorted out to your satisfaction. I'm told to talk about Hawaii.'

At the mention of Hawaii, Donna gasped. 'That's where I'm moving to,' she said.

'All will be well in Hawaii. Your mother Ellie tells me that she will be with you when you move and that is where you will find happiness and contentment and be settled.'

Donna smiled. 'Thank you so much,' she told me. 'I'm so sorry that I came here with the attitude that I did. Please accept my apologies.'

'No apologies necessary,' I told her. 'We each have our own pathway to travel and it is only when the time is right that events take place to prove to us that there is a world beyond our physical world.'

My time in California was over. It had been brief but enjoyable. I hoped that I had left a lasting impression with at least a few people and that they would remember the name 'Derek Acorah' for some time to come.

TAKING A BREAK

*F*ollowing my return from Santa Monica, being no longer required in Manchester each week to take part in *Psychic Livetime* and *Predictions with Derek Acorah*, I felt unsettled and in need of some time to think and reflect upon my future. I knew of a spiritual sanctuary in southern Spain which had been established by some light workers and mediums and decided that this would be the very place to fulfil my need for peace and reflection. Gwen was unable to accompany me, due to work commitments, but she wholeheartedly agreed that I should make the journey.

I arrived in Spain in the mid-afternoon. I had arranged a hotel for the night and was due to arrive at the sanctuary the following morning. I spent the rest of that afternoon hiring a car and contacting the sanctuary to establish the route.

The following morning I set off in the car, but soon became hopelessly lost. Anybody who knows me will confirm that I am the worst navigator in the world. Although I did arrive at the correct village, I could not find the sanctuary.

After driving around for some time I decided that the best thing to do would be to attempt to find an English-speaking person who could help me. After a couple of abortive attempts when well-meaning folk tried desperately to put me on the correct road, I eventually arrived at a bar. The owner, a lady named Rosa, was very kind. She told me that she was married to Michael, who was an Englishman. If I would care to wait ten minutes or so, he was due to return and would be able to help me find my destination.

Ten minutes or so later Michael arrived. He knew the sanctuary well and drew a detailed map for me. 'But before you go on your way I'd like to ask you a question, Derek,' he said. He pointed to a building which lay between the bar and a block of apartments and told me that a man and a woman from England had occupied the house until approximately five months previously. The whole time they had lived there strange things had occurred in the bar. Strange noises had been heard and items of crockery and cutlery were constantly being misplaced. Michael explained that he and Rosa were devoted Catholics and attended their church regularly, and although they respected my work, it was against their own personal beliefs, yet while the people had been living in the premises next door, they had had the feeling that they had been under some form of paranormal attack. Michael had enlisted the assistance of the local priest, but even having the buildings blessed had not made any difference whatsoever. He asked me if I could take a look to see whether I could throw any light on the problem.

Michael held the keys to the property and so was able to let me in to conduct an investigation. As I entered the empty house I could feel the emanations of two people in spirit. I could feel no negativity with these spirit people; in fact I would describe them as kindly souls and the atmosphere seemed to be in balance. I knew that they visited the house regularly, but sensed a vague feeling of frustration. I opened myself up to their vibrations and was able to detect that they were in fact a gentleman and a lady. They were not related but they had a common bond with Rosa and Michael.

'The spirit lady is telling me that her name is Maria Conchita Alvez,' I told Michael.

His face turned ashen. 'I'll have to call Rosa,' he said, sounding alarmed.

Upon Rosa's arrival a couple of minutes later he repeated to her what I had told him. Rosa was most upset. 'No! No!' she shouted. 'You say my grandmother is to blame for all the troubles? She is a sweet soul and is in heaven with Jesus and our Father God! Do you realize my grandmother Maria Conchita was so close to our Father God here on this Earth that her life was dedicated to helping other people? Did you know that for years she helped our village priest Father Lopez Sosa?'

In spite of Rosa's outburst, Michael asked me to continue.

'The gentleman is telling me that his name is Kenneth Baines,' I told him.

'My dad was named Kenneth and my surname is Baines,' Michael said. 'This has got to be a wind-up! You must have known about our family names. You must have known the two people who lived in this devilish place.'

I could see the disbelief in his eyes. 'All I can tell you,' I replied, 'is that I did not know either of you before I arrived at your bar, nor did I know the two people who lived in this house. If you remember, it was you who asked me to come in here. I was merely seeking directions to a sanctuary, which, if what you tell me is correct, is eight or more miles away from here. Did the people who lived here know your father's name? Did they know that he had cancer in his lung, that he had to have his left leg amputated? Did they know Rosa's grandmother's name?'

Michael and Rosa looked at each other. They had to admit that they had never spoken to the two people who had shared the house. They had been solitary souls and did not mix with the local people.

Michael dropped his eyes and apologized. 'I'm sorry, Derek,' he said, 'but it's difficult for us to come to terms with the fact that my father and Rosa's grandmother are not at peace in heaven with God. My father did not know Rosa's grandmother—they never met. How is it that they have come here together?'

I explained that though the two spirit people had not known each other here on this Earth, they had met in the spirit world, or heaven, or whatever people wish to call the higher side of life. They had been drawn to each other because they were like-minded souls, both being deeply religious and having a great faith in God. Furthermore, because Michael and Rosa had married, they had a common bond. They had visited the bar to try to draw attention to the fact that they were around and taking an interest in Michael's and Rosa's lives. They wanted them both to know that they were happy and at peace in the world of spirit.

'Thank you, Derek,' Michael told me. 'You have given Rosa and me a deeper understanding of the work that you do. We know now that it's not the Devil's work but merely a different perspective.'

I said my goodbyes. Following Michael's directions, I finally arrived at the sanctuary—some three hours late, but it had been worth it. From fearing my work, Michael and Rosa had expanded their minds and accepted that mediums are not bad people after all.

MOST HAUNTED
INVESTIGATIONS

A SECOND VISIT TO TUTBURY

The whole point of *Most Haunted* investigations is that I know nothing about the location I am to visit. So when the *Most Haunted* crew followed the researcher's car through the winding Staffordshire lanes and drew up in front of the gates of the castle, I was horrified. I explained to Karl that I had been there before as part of a *Predictions* investigation, but he told me, 'We know that you won't use any prior knowledge and that you'll only talk about what you're receiving tonight.'

Of course Karl was correct. As a medium I will only give off what I am receiving at the time. And although the residual energies of a place will remain the same, it would be impossible for any spirit visitation or messages from spirit to be identical on different occasions. For instance, Mary Queen of Scots travelled around extensively and although the residual energy of her occupation of various buildings will always remain, her spirit body can only be in one place at any particular time. In spirit the same rule applies as in life: we can only be in one place at once.

As I arrived at Tutbury, Lesley was in the house waiting to greet me, though this time minus her Mary Queen of Scots costume. I hardly recognized her! The rest of the crew had been at the castle all day and were excited at the prospect of the forthcoming investigation.

We began in the Great Hall. Once more Charles I paid a fleeting visit, this time accompanied by his nephew Rupert. I sensed talk of battle prevailing between the two.

Then a darker male spirit entered the room. The atmosphere changed to one of mean-spiritedness. I did not like the emanations of the man. 'Amyas Paulet,' announced Sam. I could see Richard Felix behind the cameras smiling and nodding. I had no clue as to who this Amyas Paulet was; what I did know was that he had been a mean-minded and nasty individual in his physical life. This was later validated by Richard, who explained that Amyas Paulet had been the person who was charged with the guardianship of Mary Queen of Scots whilst she was imprisoned at Tutbury castle. He was a particularly nasty person who insisted on keeping Mary under close arrest and would not allow her many of the favours which she had enjoyed previously, for fear of upsetting Queen Elizabeth I.

Our investigation continued. The cold spot or vortex in the small room was still there, though Edmund, Earl of Lancaster, was not in evidence. The residual energy of his personality remained, however, in the room at the top of the stairs.

Out in the dark night Yvette, Phil and I trudged up the slippery wooden steps to the ruined remains of the motte. I knew immediately that here, beneath my feet, were the physical remains of many people—people who had died in agony. Below the ground was an oubliette—a hole in the ground into which people would be thrown to await a painful and lingering passing to spirit. They would have no food or water and their wounds and broken bones would remain untended. The suffering of the people who had been left to die here permeated the night air and assailed my senses. I could stay no longer. I stumbled down the steps to return to the house.

Once again I visited the chapel and climbed the north tower, and once again I experienced the energy of the medieval soldier as he rushed down the steps. Then I walked through the Queen's Garden and went down the steps to the remains of the cellars of what would long ago have been the king's lodgings. The floors of the building have long gone. All that remains are the holes in the walls where the joists which supported the floor had been located and the empty yawning fireplace. The roof has gone and the interior is open to the elements. At the level of what would have been the first floor I noticed a movement. I looked up and saw a doorway. I could see the spirit form of a monk standing there. 'I have to go up there, Karl' I said.

Karl looked at me doubtfully. 'Are you sure? It's a long way up!'

I had forgotten in my eagerness that I am not too good with heights at all. At the time Karl was unaware of this. He was merely considering the physical difficulties.

A ladder was brought and I started my ascent with Karl following me, holding a camera. We reached the doorway and discovered a small stone passageway. I could vaguely discern the outline of the hooded monk. 'This is Thomas,' Sam told me. 'He often returns to these quarters. He comes in memory of the days when he served his king here.'

We took our first tentative steps in Thomas's direction. The pigeons who for years had been using the corridor as a roost started cooing and moving, flapping their wings in indignation and making attempts to escape through the only exit—the doorway by which we had entered. It was no good. We had to go back. The only problem was, having climbed up the ladder quite easily, now, as I looked down in the torchlight to the ground far below, I froze. I just could not bring myself to make the journey back down the ladder. Thank goodness for Karl. His common sense and calmness helped me, step by step, to make it back to ground level. I really do not know what I would have done without him. The rest of the crew found it hilarious. It took me quite some time to live that particular incident down.

The investigation continued, followed by the vigils when Yvette and Phil experienced rapping sounds on the windows which terrified the life out of them. By the end of the night we felt happy that a thorough investigation of Tutbury had been completed and although only sounds had been recorded, we could confirm that the old castle is indeed home to many inexplicable events. As a medium, I can say that as well as the obvious abundance of residual energy, there are also many people in spirit who make their way back to visit Tutbury castle.

My two separate investigations at Tutbury demonstrate the fact that although residual energies remain, the spirit presence at any given time can be very different.

BELGRAVE HALL

There was a second time when *Most Haunted* visited a location in which I had previously conducted an investigation, in this case Belgrave Hall in Leicestershire. My first visit there had been with the ISPR team. This time I had been downloading e-mails when I had come across one from a woman called Nancy. She wrote that she and her husband were avid viewers of *Most Haunted* and would both love the opportunity of joining the *Most Haunted* crew on an investigation. Oh, and by the way, her husband was none other than Vic Reeves, one half of the comic duo Reeves and Mortimer.

I was proud and not a little flattered that the famous Vic Reeves would take time out to view a programme in which I was involved. I passed the e-mail on to Karl, who extended an invitation for Nancy and Vic to take part in a programme.

It was a beautiful day in July when I arrived at Belgrave. Once again I had to point out that I had visited the location on a previous occasion. Once again Karl patted me on the shoulder and told me that he knew that I would speak only about the spirits who happened to be at the hall at the time of our visit. I was introduced to Nancy and Vic, who told me that they were both a little nervous but were looking forward to taking part. Vic confided to me that he believed that he had seen and heard 'ghosts', as he called them, throughout his life. I was not at all surprised to hear this, as I knew upon meeting him that as well as his quick wit and sense of humour he had a highly developed intuition and sensitivity.

The day was long and warm and we had to wait until quite late in the evening before we could commence filming. We returned to the hall from supper around 9:30. Darkness was falling and in the half-light the old hall seemed to have changed. Now there was a brooding atmosphere, almost as though the spirits of Belgrave were waiting for us. 'The whole place seems to be pulsating,' somebody commented. It was certainly different from the first time I had visited.

As I entered the hall from the back garden door I could sense a man's energy on the stairs which rose up to the left of me. He gave the impression of somebody who was old and who had been a servant. I had the impression that an accident had occurred, that he had fallen down those very stairs and had passed to spirit as a result of that fall. Though I was only picking up residual energy, Sam told me that the man's spirit did at times visit the hall and wander around both the ground and upper floors.

As on the occasion of my first visit, I could detect a female energy and had the impression of Victoriana. The spirit form of a lady appeared briefly on the staircase.

The investigation continued throughout the house. On the upper floor I was strongly impressed by the spirit of a man who announced himself as Edmund Craddock. As on my first visit, Edmund resented the invasion of the place which he still considered belonged to him. He was prepared to put up with daytime visitors but was not at all willing to have his home 'despoiled', as he put it, during the evening and night-time hours. I once again picked up feelings of anger and negativity with this man.

When we reached the nursery we decided to sit quietly to see if anybody from spirit would decide to show themselves. I knew that activity had been experienced here but at the moment there was nothing more than residual energy.

We had been sitting in the room for a while when Tom announced that the battery on his sound equipment had inexplicably drained. A loud bang was heard and then a click. We sat expectantly. After a few moments Rick began to complain that he felt unwell.

'Maybe it would be wise to take Rick out for a breath of fresh air,' I suggested. Karl agreed and proceeded to help Rick down the stairs and out into the garden.

Upon Karl's return the vigil continued, but after a while Yvette suggested that we move on to another room, as nothing seemed to be happening in the nursery. We were just about to move on when we heard the thunder of feet on the staircase. Stuart burst through the nursery door. 'Rick and I have just seen a ghost down in the garden!' he shouted.

We all ran down the stairs and out into the garden. A very white-faced newspaper reporter was standing shaking in the middle of the lawn. 'I saw it too,' she said.

Stuart and Rick excitedly told us what they had seen. They had been sitting on a garden bench when their attention had been caught by a movement over at the side of the garden on the path which runs next to a herbaceous border underneath the high garden wall. They were unable to distinguish whether it had been a male or female figure but described it as being 'a thinnish shape—a possible side profile'. I was sure that they were both convinced that they had seen something, though by the time we arrived at the garden there was definitely no trace of spiritual activity. Richard Felix walked up and down the pathway with a crystal pendulum, following the route which Stuart and Rick said the entity had taken. Pendulums are often used to detect the presence of spirit activity. It is a form of dowsing. In this case the crystal remained static. Yvette voiced the opinion that she did not believe that dowsing was ever successful, but I have to disagree with her on this point, as I have seen crystal dowsing work very successfully.

After all this excitement we split into small groups and roamed from room to room to see if we could hear or sense anything other than the very physical creaks and groans of the old house. When we met up once more in the hallway, we found that nothing paranormal had taken place.

Vic asked whether he could take a wander around on his own with a camera. After a very short time we heard a yell and he came tumbling down the stairs. He reported that he had heard two creaks and a loud bang, but then decided that the noises had probably been normal after all and that there had been nothing 'spooky' about them.

We all trooped up the stairs once more and sat quietly for a while. We had to agree that Vic had probably over-reacted to nothing more than the sounds of settlement. 'What about a séance?' suggested Yvette, looking around the group.

As the downstairs hallway had the largest space free of furniture, chairs were brought and arranged to form a circle there. We all sat down with joined hands. The people who were not taking part in the séance sat on the stairs. There was complete silence. I opened myself up to spirit influence once more. I knew that the angry spirit of Edmund Craddock had not gone away but lingered close at hand. I breathed in deeply and exhaled. I could feel the spirit of Edmund drawing closer and closer. I was not prepared to allow this spirit person to completely overshadow me, but he was strong and was equally determined. Gwen told me later that a real battle appeared to be waging between us and at one point I banged my head against the wall of the hallway. Finally, I stood up and made a lunging motion towards Stuart and it seemed that I had stopped breathing. As nobody appeared to be doing anything to help me, Gwen felt compelled at this point to run in and command me to breathe. At the same time she gave me a jolt in the ribs to make me draw breath.

Karl helped me outside. 'I think it would be unwise for a séance to continue,' I told him. Yvette, however, wanted to carry on. 'OK,' I said, 'if you want to continue, that's up to you, but I know that Edmund's spirit is determined to cause problems. Although I don't wish to take part in the next séance, I will be here a few feet away on the other side of the door.'

As I stood enjoying a cigarette I told Gwen and one of the reporters that I knew the crew would experience problems. Even as I said this, I could hear Yvette's voice asking Edmund to communicate with the group. No sooner had she spoken than it sounded as though pandemonium had broken loose inside the hallway. I thrust open the door. John was sitting rigidly and appeared to be very dazed. He was staring blankly ahead. Rick was complaining that John was gripping his fingers so tightly that he was losing the feeling in them. Rick was also shouting that he could feel breathing on his hand. Yvette was shouting to people to look at her lower legs. They were being raised, as though by unseen hands, so that they were almost vertical with the level of her thighs as she sat on her chair. Karl, next to whom I was standing, suddenly slumped onto the floor. I helped him up and took him outside and out of the atmosphere of Edmund Craddock, whom I could see grinning maliciously as he enjoyed the mayhem he had caused.

I returned to the hallway to help in getting John outside. His legs had become weak and totally useless. As

Richard, Stuart and I were assisting John, we heard Vic let out a yell. He made a dive for the staircase and raced up the stairs, shouting and yelling at the malicious entity as he went. 'Go away!' he yelled as he raced along the corridor. 'Go away! Leave us alone!'

He returned down the stairs shaking his head. 'I knew there was something or somebody there,' he said. Of course he did! Vic is very sensitive and although he may not have been able to define exactly who the spirit was, I knew that he was empathic enough to be aware that there was spirit presence and that the presence was not a friendly one.

Everybody decided that enough was enough. Dawn was streaking the sky and it was time to head off to the hotel for a well-earned rest.

Belgrave Hall is considered to be one of the most haunted locations in Britain today. I think that the Most Haunted crew's night there with Vic Reeves and Nancy Sorrell certainly proved that.

LEAP CASTLE

One of the strangest experiences I have encountered during my investigations of haunted locations is when I went with the Most Haunted crew to Ireland to visit Leap castle.

Leap is almost completely ruined. All that remains of the old castle is a tower and in this tower lives the owner, Sean, together with his wife and daughter.

The investigation had progressed well and we had taken a short break during the proceedings to eat dinner. While we were doing so, Sean's daughter had given a demonstration of

Irish dancing, at which she was truly adept, with Sean accompanying her on the tin whistle. It was a beautiful experience sitting in front of the enormous log fire whilst the soulful notes of the whistle echoed through the old stone rooms.

It was drawing close to midnight and time to recommence our investigation. We walked up the circular stone staircase to the first floor of the castle. Sean accompanied us to watch the proceedings. As we entered the room he took a seat on a chair in the corner. I noticed a movement on a small gallery which looked down over us. As I looked up I could see a lady in spirit. She was beautiful—tall and slim with long black hair, and wearing a flowing red gown.

'We must go up to the gallery,' I told the crew. 'I can see activity up there!'

By the time we reached the small gallery, the spirit lady had disappeared, but as I stood talking to Yvette about what I had seen I became aware of the most horrible stench. Words cannot describe how awful the smell was. I looked to my left and was shocked to see a creature which almost defies description. It seemed to be a mixture of a human being and an ape.

As I started telling Yvette what I was seeing I heard Sean shout from the room below, 'Don't, Derek! Stop! I don't want you to continue.'

I stopped speaking. As I did so, the creature slowly appeared to dissolve into the ether and in its place stood the beautiful lady dressed in red once more. Was this shapeshifting? I had long been dubious about the stories of shapeshifters, but now I had to change my mind. Sam was telling me that the lady had lived in Leap castle many years ago. She had been known to practise the black arts and had become so skilled in them that she had learned to shape-shift: to appear as herself one moment and then to transform herself into the gruesome creature I had witnessed moments before.

In the room below Sean was becoming very agitated. He explained that the monster was known to inhabit the castle but that it had not been seen for many years. Quite understandably, he did not wish its energies to be summoned up once more, as he and his family lived there. I quite understood and abandoned this part of the investigation, but I don't think I will ever forget my one and only meeting with a shape-shifting spirit.

The Auric Field

On occasions I have been criticized following programmes in the *Most Haunted* series because of my
willingness to allow certain spirit entities to enter my auric
field and 'take over' my physical body.

The aura is an energy field surrounding the physical body.
It contains a mixture of colours which show both your physical and emotional well-being and your state of progress as a
spirit in a physical body. The colours to do with your emotions and health change frequently, while the colours denot-
ing your level of spirituality do not.

A spirit person can only draw close to you and enter this
energy field if you allow it to do so. If a medium channels a
spirit by allowing that spirit person to enter their aura, they
do it of their own free will. No spirit person can force such
an event to take place. The power is with the medium or
host. Mediums are, however, only human and can misjudge
a situation. They can be taken by surprise in a moment of
lost concentration, they can fall prey to the blandishments

of a spirit person who may have been an adept confidence trickster when in their physical life, or they can misjudge the strength of the spirit person with whom they are dealing. Although we all have our guides to help us, it is personal choice which ultimately takes precedence.

A number of instances of this spring to mind, the most memorable being the incidents that took place at Brannigans nightclub in Manchester and at the House of Detention in Clerkenwell, London.

BRANNIGANS

On entering Brannigans nightclub I was unaware that the building had once been the Albert Hall, home of the Manchester & Salford Methodist Mission. Above the room full of music and dazzling disco lights, the main hall of the church still remained, complete with huge church organ.

Before commencing the *Most Haunted* investigation Karl had taken me around the hall and into the small rooms which led from the main area. As I walked around I became more and more aware that within the precincts of the building lurked a malevolent spirit who resented our intrusion into his world. There were other spirits present and the atmosphere burgeoned with the residual energy of the times when people used to gather there to pray and even of the children who had been cared for by the deaconesses. I knew that great acts of selflessness and sacrifice had taken place. But I also knew that alongside this spirituality ran something darker.

As Karl and I roamed the area behind the pipes of the great organ we decided to climb up to a higher level. I was nervous of doing this as I had a feeling of uneasiness in the area, but nonetheless I continued upwards.

As we reached a point approximately halfway up, Karl suddenly slipped. Had he fallen, he would most certainly have been seriously hurt, but luckily I managed to grasp his wrist whilst he re-established his footing.

'We should go back,' I told him. I knew that the malevolent spirit would try his best to harm us if we gave him the slightest opportunity. We returned to the area in the main hall where the rest of the crew were gathered.

I had established that should I allow the spirit of the man who ruled Brannigans to enter my aura I would be taking a very great risk indeed. He was a strong spirit, as shown by the fact that he had already managed to cause Karl to lose his footing. On the other hand I knew that I had Sam to protect me. I also had the power of choice.

The investigation at Brannigans proceeded and we decided that we would go up to the clock tower. Access to this tower is via a vertical ladder which is attached to the wall and which emerges into a small area just outside the clock tower. Having reached the top of the ladder I entered the tower room. It was quite small, very dark and contained what I can only describe as a stone trough which ran down the centre. To say that space was limited would be an understatement.

The cameras rolled and I could feel a spirit drawing near to me. I felt quite strong and well in control of the situation. The spirit form of a man drew closer and closer. I was still happy to allow this proximity, though I knew that the person, when in life, had not been the nicest of people. It was completely dark. All I could see were the tiny red lights of the cameras and the faintly illuminated faces of the people holding them. I was relating to Yvette what I was being told by Sam. I decided that I would allow the spirit to enter my aura.

I can only relate what crew members have told me about the events which now took place. I was told that I proceeded to become most arrogant and belligerent. I strutted up and down in front of them and took on a menacing air, appearing to be completely sure of my footing, even though it was impossible to see any hazards. On viewing the footage at a later date I could see the nervousness on the faces of crew members, especially poor Tom, whose sound equipment I decided to poke around at.

Then I suddenly leaped a foot or two upwards into the raised doorway of a small ante-room. I walked around the room, then reappeared in that same doorway. Gwen tells me that it was at this point that she knew things were going too far and that I had to be recalled to take complete control of myself. I was approaching Rick in such a threatening manner that she was afraid I was going to become violent towards him.

As Gwen started to shout my name, Karl rushed forward and took hold of me. I collapsed into his arms. He lowered me onto the edge of the stone trough. I had no feeling in my legs at all. It was with great difficulty that I was manhandled out of the room, down the vertical ladder and back into the main hall.

What had happened? I had allowed the spirit to enter my aura. It was only when he had overshadowed me completely that I had realized his actual strength. I had not experienced this volume of strength in a spirit before and it had taken more than a little effort to regain control of myself. Put simply, I had misjudged the situation. As I mentioned earlier, we mediums are only human and can make mistakes.

After this incident, my energies were totally depleted. Four days later I still had areas of numbness in my legs, but the feeling returned within five or six days and there were no lasting ill effects.

AT THE HOUSE OF DETENTION

Another example of when I was taken unawares by a spirit person was during the *Most Haunted* crew's investigation of the House of Detention in Clerkenwell, London.

At first everything had gone well. The joint investigation with all the crew members had taken place. I had related the harrowing tale of prison life in the 1800s, including the fact that children were incarcerated there in those days. There was one particular small girl whose heart-rending sobs could be heard reverberating around the jail. There was also the spirit of an old lady who seemed to be perpetually searching for something or somebody.

The time had come when we were to split into separate groups. Because I had detected a particularly malevolent spirit whose revolting descriptions of what he liked to do to womenfolk had stunned me, it was decided that one group at a time would go out into the passageways. The remainder of the crew would stay together in the room which we had set aside for storing equipment.

Yvette, Phil and I were the first group to venture into the maze-like tunnels and corridors. Because of the condition of the floor—some parts having been removed, leaving hazardous holes—Phil carried a torch.

As we entered a chamber at the rear of the premises it was obvious to me that we were not alone. The malevolent spirit had joined us. I felt him draw closer. Sam was warning me to take care.

Suddenly, to my horror, Sam's voice faded. I desperately tried to hear him but his voice was diminishing rapidly and I lost communication with him completely. In that moment of lost concentration, because I had allowed the spirit to draw so close to me, he attempted to overshadow me completely. I felt myself being thrown upwards and backwards. I could vaguely hear Yvette screaming, 'Karl! Karl!' With a monumental effort I repelled the spirit, sending him backwards and away from us. I felt weakened and dazed.

After what seemed a very long time Karl appeared.

'Didn't you hear me on the radio?' Yvette asked him.

'No,' Karl replied. 'We didn't hear you on the radio at all. I heard your voice faintly shouting for me from the tunnels and I came running.'

The malevolent male spirit had obviously managed to tamper with the radio equipment, thus attempting to prevent communication between us. Thank goodness for Yvette's lung power!

Once again I had been caught off my guard and a less than kindred spirit had taken the opportunity to step into my aura in an attempt to create problems.

It must be remembered, though, that although momentary mischief can be caused by a spirit entity, ultimately they cannot take us over. Complete possession of a medium is just not possible.

WARWICK CASTLE

I had been filming for *Most Haunted* at Llancaiach Fawr Manor in the heart of Caerphilly. Over the 24 hours of the filming it had snowed hard and I had been beginning to think that I would be forced to spend a couple of days there with the ghosts of the Prichard family and would be unable to fulfil my commitment to take part in the BBC programme *I'll Do Anything*.

I'll Do Anything is a programme hosted by the ex-footballer Ian Wright. Contestants write in to the television company in an effort to be selected to take part in a challenge. If they complete their set task, their prize is the granting of the wish of a loved one.

The task in which I was to take part involved Patricia, who would be spending a night 'alone' in Warwick Castle. She was to stay there for seven hours, from midnight through to 7 o'clock in the morning, spending a full hour in each of the castle's most haunted locations. It was her husband's dearest wish to experience a dream holiday in

Florida and this brave lady was prepared to take on the task to make his dream come true. It was my task to take Patricia around the seven locations, giving her the benefit of what I was picking up through my mediumship in a couple of the 'most haunted' places.

We started off in the Great Hall, which is dominated by life-size statues of two horses and riders in full armour, ready for battle. We continued on through the corridors, drawing rooms and boudoirs and on to the Kenilworth Room. Many royal guests have stayed at Warwick, including King Edward VII, who was a frequent visitor before he ascended to the throne, and a weekend visit has been recreated in several of the rooms, with wax models of the regal visitors. Consequently, wherever we went we were met by these heart-stoppingly lifelike models.

We finally reached the Ghost Tower, which is where the body of the poet and dramatist Sir Fulke Greville, a former owner of the castle, was brought after he had been stabbed to death by his manservant in London. As Patricia and I entered the bedchamber which was to be the last resting-place of Sir Fulke Greville's earthly body, I could sense that much spirit activity had been experienced here. I was drawn towards the bed and as I reached out my arm I could feel the temperature begin to drop. I heard a rustling sound and looked towards a chair which stood next to the bed. Gradually, the spirit form of a man began to develop. As he became clearer to me, I could see that he was attired in Elizabethan dress. But as soon as he appeared, he began to fade from my sight. I was merely being allowed a brief glimpse of the man who had occupied this room during his life here on Earth.

I walked over to the chair. The air surrounding it was considerably cooler than the rest of the room.

I called Patricia over. 'Sit in this chair and tell me what you feel,' I said.

Patricia sat down. 'Ooooh!' she said. 'It's cold and it feels tingly!'

'That's because Sir Fulke Greville has just paid us a brief visit,' I told her.

She visibly paled at this piece of information. 'I don't know whether I'll be able to do this,' I heard her mutter to herself.

Our final destination was the dungeon, where prisoners would endure days, weeks and months in the small dark space. The air was heavy with the atmosphere of past sufferings. I felt bombarded by the general feeling of misery as I moved further into the dank cells towards an oubliette—a stone-lined pit sunk into the ground into which prisoners would once have been thrown and left to die. This was the very worst type of incarceration. I felt sickened at the atmosphere but because I knew that Patricia was determined to win the holiday of a lifetime for her husband, I said nothing, but allowing her to absorb the emanations of the dungeon herself. It would be bad enough for her without me describing the horrors which had once taken place in these smelly rooms.

We returned to the Great Hall. 'D'you think I'll do it, Derek?' Patricia asked me.

'Of course you will,' I told her, but I knew that it would not be easy.

The challenge commenced. Patricia was left in the Great Hall on her own. At the end of each hour a hooded monk would appear and silently beckon her on to the next room. By 4 o'clock in the morning I was beginning to feel so sorry for her. She was truly terrified out of her wits. She had thrown the hood of her jacket over her head, put her head on her arms and started sobbing with fright—and she still had three more locations to visit.

'D'you think she'll make it, Derek?' asked the producer.

'She will,' I replied. 'That lady's made of stern stuff and she's determined that her husband's wish will be granted.'

Another hour dragged by. Six o'clock came and it was time to go back to the Great Hall. Patricia had only one hour to go to complete the task. As she sat at the long table I could see that she had had enough and that it would take an enormous amount of willpower for her to stay there and not sound the klaxon which would herald her decision that she was unable to carry on. 'Come on!' I whispered to myself. 'You can do it!'

The fingers on the clock in the temporary studio seemed to creep around to that magical hour of 7 o'clock in the morning. At last the minute finger hit 12.

'Go and get her, Derek!' shouted the location producer.

I raced down the corridor and threw open the door to the Great Hall. 'You've done it!' I shouted. 'You've won!'

'Oh Derek!' said Patricia as she ran towards me and threw her arms around me. 'Thank goodness it's over!' she sobbed.

'I knew you'd make it,' I told her.

I have to say that Patricia is one of the bravest people I have ever met. It is all very well to go into haunted locations with a group of people to conduct investigations, but it takes a special type of person to spend seven hours alone with only your imagination for company. What nobody had reckoned on, however, was Patricia's love for her husband Roger. She was determined to win the dream holiday for him. He's a very lucky man indeed.

KILROY

O ver the years I have been invited several times to appear as a guest on Robert Kilroy's morning programme, where I have enjoyed healthy debate with other guests, both those who are sceptical of the gift of mediumship and those who believe wholeheartedly in communication with the world of spirit.

I would describe Robert Kilroy Silk as an open-minded sceptic who does a good job of flushing out the charlatans but quite readily admits that his own grandmother 'read the tea leaves'. It was during one particularly lively debate that he turned to me with a wicked glint in his eye and said, 'Well, Derek Acorah! You don't know Barbara, but she knows of you!'

The cameras panned around to focus on a young lady in the audience whom I certainly did not recognize. I must have looked surprised, because Robert laughingly added, 'You look worried! You're wondering what she's going to say! Go on, Barbara. Tell him.'

Barbara then proceeded to tell me that her husband had been for a sitting at my office in Liverpool. He was then married to someone else. He had gone along to consult me because he was unhappy in his work and was wondering whether I could see any changes ahead for him. I had apparently told him that he would be leaving his present place of work and would be taking up a job in London. At the time he had no intention whatsoever of relocating to another part of the country. I had also told him that I could see changes in his emotional life, that his current relationship would founder and that he would meet and marry a young lady named 'Barbara' whilst living and working in the London region.

Barbara said that her husband had been deeply sceptical about what I had to tell him, especially when I had mentioned a second marriage. He had left my office thinking that his trip to see me had been a complete waste of time and money. How wrong he turned out to be! Within months of his consultation with me his first marriage had come to an end and he had sought work with another company. That company had relocated him to London and some months later he had met and married Barbara.

Robert informed the audience that he had not intentionally brought Barbara onto his programme for the purpose of relating her story, but that one of his researchers had overheard a conversation she had been having with another audience member and they thought they would surprise me with her story live on air.

'I WAS GOBSMACKED'

I can recall another occasion during a *Kilroy* programme when my heart was made to flutter. Again, the subject of the day was psychics and mediums. I had been invited to appear with Yvette Fielding to represent *Most Haunted*.

Debate was brisk, with one particularly sceptical gentleman holding the floor. One or two other equally sceptical audience members were also putting forward their points of view and things were not looking very good for psychics.

The microphone was passed to one jovial Liverpudlian chap who had put up his hand to make a point. 'Well,' he said, 'I don't believe in psychics and mediums generally. I've spent thousands of pounds visiting them to try and find answers, but I consider that they've all been a waste of money.'

With the man having such a broad Liverpudlian accent all eyes turned scathingly in my direction, as it was more or less obvious that he would have at some time consulted me.

'However,' he continued, 'there's one psychic I did visit and I was gobsmacked when everything he told me turned out to be true. That psychic was Derek Acorah.' He turned and pointed to me. 'I went to see Derek when he had his office in Liverpool. I was desperate for a job as I'd been out of work for a long time and I thought I'd give him a try to see whether there was anything in the pipeline for me. He told me that I'd see a job in the *Echo*. He told me to apply for the job and I'd get it!' (The *Liverpool Echo* is a local newspaper.) The man laughed as he added, 'Anybody from Liverpool knows that it's hopeless looking for a job in the

Echo because there are never any ordinary ones advertised. Derek told me that the job would be out of the Liverpool area and that I would be working and living next to playing fields and a park. He told me that I would be very happy in my job and that it would be a long-term appointment. I went away thinking, "Another waste of money," but nonetheless looked in the sits vac column on the Thursday just as Derek had told me. Lo and behold, there was a job advertised which suited me, so I applied for it and got it. Just as Derek had told me, it was out of the Liverpool area. It was a school caretaker's job and part of that job included caring for the playing fields. My house is in a park next to the playing fields. I'm really very happy with the job and I've been doing it ever since.'

Once again I breathed a huge sigh of relief!

From Euston to Liverpool

I had just appeared on LIVINGtv's programme *Loose Lips*, hosted by Richard Arnold and Melinda Messenger, and was due at Euston station in London to catch the 7 p.m. train back to Lime Street station in Liverpool. *Loose Lips* is a magazine-style daytime programme and I had been asked to go along to talk about my experiences on *Most Haunted* and my life as a medium in general. Everything had gone well and I had arrived at the station with a few minutes to spare.

As I was making my way to platform 7, a young man approached me. 'Are you Derek Acorah?' I said that I was. 'Great to meet you in the flesh. Would you do me a favour and speak to one of your biggest fans?'

I glanced at my watch. 'I'm actually in a tremendous hurry as I have to catch a train,' I told him, 'but I will speak for a moment.'

I took the telephone from him and heard a lady's voice asking who it was. I told her that it was Derek Acorah.

'Never! You're kidding me! Paul's winding me up!' she shouted.

Paul reached for the telephone. 'Don't put the phone down, Lisa. It really is Derek Acorah.' He handed the telephone back to me.

'Can I ask you a very important question, Derek?' she asked. 'Tell me if it's not possible.'

I told her that I was just about to catch a train, but if she would give me her telephone number I would give her a call as soon as I was on board. I said a hurried 'goodbye' to Paul and sprinted down the platform, jumping onto the train with only a moment or two to spare.

After I had settled myself down in a vacant seat I picked up my telephone and dialed Lisa's number.

'Thanks so much for contacting me, Derek,' she said. 'I wanted to speak to you because at the moment my dad Graham is quite ill in hospital undergoing tests. Will he be OK, Derek? I couldn't cope if anything was to happen to him. We lost Mum just two short years ago and we're still trying to come to terms with that.'

When I opened myself up mentally to Lisa's question, I quickly became aware of a spirit person who had drawn close to me; a man with what seemed to be chronic chest pain. He seemed to be somewhat bewildered and he had a problem with his left leg. I tried to communicate with him, but I was finding it impossible, so Sam stepped in. Sam told me that the man in spirit was Lisa's father, Graham, that he had left this physical world less than 30 minutes earlier and that he was concerned that his daughter had not received a telephone call from the hospital.

I was shocked. Here I was talking on the telephone to Lisa and she was unaware that her father had passed to the spirit world.

'Are you at home, Lisa?' I asked her. She told me no, she was at her friend Andrea's house. 'I feel that you should contact the hospital immediately,' I told her. Lisa promised that she would and hung up.

A few moments later my mobile telephone rang again. It was Paul. He asked whether I had managed to catch my train and thanked me for speaking to Lisa. He told me that she had been in touch with him and instead of telephoning the hospital had jumped into her car and had driven directly to the hospital.

I leaned wearily back into my seat. As I closed my eyes I became aware of the man in spirit who I now knew to be Lisa's father. Sam was again acting as communicator. He told me that Graham had been met by his mother, father and grandmother as he passed to the world of spirit, but his greatest thrill was to be reunited with his beloved wife Jane. He was so excited and wanted Lisa and Paul to know that their parents were reunited and not to worry. I was pleased to hear of the reunion, but I was saddened to contemplate the shock which Lisa and Paul would have to endure.

The ringing of the mobile telephone broke into my thoughts. It was Lisa. She was sobbing. 'Derek, my dad is dead. He has died. I cannot believe it. I knew he was ill, but I thought he would come out of hospital and come home again. What you said when you asked me to telephone the hospital—did you know? I must know this!'

I explained to Lisa as gently as possible that her dad had come to me earlier when I was speaking to her. I told her that her father wanted to pass on his love to her, to Paul and to his other son, who was also called Graham. I told her that he had been reunited with their mother Jane and that they were both at peace in the spirit world.

Lisa was heartbroken. She told me that when she had arrived at the hospital they had told her that they had been trying to contact her for almost two hours but had not been able to do so. She felt so guilty at missing her father's last moments here on Earth.

'Don't feel guilty,' I advised her. 'There is no need. Your father was met by his mother and father and your lovely mum. They knew that he was ready to be received into God's kingdom. I know it is the most horrible thing to experience the loss of a parent, but you have your life ahead of you and your mum and dad will always be around you. They'll celebrate the good things in your life with you and they'll be there to help you through the harder times. What you must remember is that they are not lost to you.'

'Thank you, Derek,' Lisa said. 'D'you think that Paul was meant to bump into you on Euston station?'

'I think there's a very strong possibility!' I replied.

LADY ON THE SHIP

In the summer of 2002 Gwen and I were fortunate enough to be able to spend a holiday on board a ship cruising around the Mediterranean. It was during this holiday that I experienced a situation that was entirely new to me.

In my work as a spirit medium I follow a strict discipline of opening myself up to the spirit realms whilst working and then closing myself down when that work is complete. This is a discipline followed by all responsible mediums. If we left ourselves open to spirit influences all the time, we would certainly experience problems.

We had been on board the ship for a day or two and I was enjoying my breakfast on deck when I suddenly heard a voice which I knew was coming from the realms of spirit. 'I'm Jimmy,' it said in a strong Glaswegian accent. 'My wife's on this ship and I want you to tell her that I'm OK now!'

How on earth could I do that? First, I didn't know who Jimmy's wife was—I was on board a ship with almost 1,000 holidaying passengers—and secondly, it is against all the rules and ethics of mediumship to just approach a total stranger out of the blue with a message from a loved one who has passed to spirit, as this is a gross invasion of a person's privacy. It was not something that I was prepared to do.

'Stand back!' I commanded and mentally went through my closing-down procedure.

I told Gwen what had happened. 'You can't just go up to a total stranger and tell them that you've been speaking to their husband in spirit,' she said. 'Apart from anything else, they may think you're completely bonkers and have you arrested. Tell the chap to leave you alone!'

Unfortunately Jimmy wouldn't take no for an answer. For the rest of the day he kept creeping into my consciousness and talking to me, pleading with me to let his wife know that he was 'alright now'. The situation was becoming ridiculous.

As we were walking down to the ship's restaurant for our evening meal, suddenly Jimmy was back with me again. 'There she is!' he shouted excitedly. 'There's my wife in the green top!'

I looked and could see a lady in her thirties walking along in the company of an older lady and another of about her own age and a boy who looked to be about 10 or 11.

'That's my son Paul,' Jimmy said proudly. 'Please speak to Mary and let her know I'm OK.'

I tried to ignore Jimmy, but throughout the evening he kept on asking me to speak to his wife and strangely, no matter where Gwen and I went on the ship, we found that we kept bumping into her. I knew that the only way I would be left to enjoy my holiday in peace was to approach Jimmy's wife and pass his message on. But how to do it?

I asked Gwen, who was no help whatsoever. She repeated what she'd said earlier and I have to say that I agreed with her. But Jimmy was still pleading with me to speak to his wife.

After dinner we were sitting in a lounge having coffee when I noticed that Jimmy's wife and her group were sitting at a table not too far away from us. The older lady had stood up. I thought to myself that if I went over to her, away from Jimmy's wife, told her that I was a spirit medium and explained my predicament regarding Jimmy, she might just be understanding enough to ask Jimmy's wife whether she would mind if I spoke to her.

I walked over and spoke to her. After a moment, she nodded and said, 'I'll ask her.' She walked over to Jimmy's wife and whispered to her. Then I saw her look over and nod.

I drew a deep breath and started to tell Jimmy's wife what Jimmy was saying to me: that he was sorry; he had made a mistake and hadn't meant to take himself over to the world of spirit. The drugs he had taken had been tampered with. He named the people he had been mixing with.

'I know that already,' said Mary with tears in her eyes.

I told her that Jimmy loved the tattoo she'd had done.

She laughed and said, 'Tell him I'll never stop loving him. He's my husband and always will be.'

'He's met John,' I told her. 'He was the first person he saw when he passed over to spirit.'

'That's his dad,' she said. 'He missed him so much; he was heartbroken when he lost him. I'm so pleased they're back together again.'

Jimmy went on to talk about the spirit people he'd met: a friend who had been involved in an accident, a dog he'd had as a child. He spoke of his mother Enid and other members of his family with whom he had been reunited.

Mary took hold of my hand. 'Thank you,' she said, 'thank you so much for sharing your gift with me. I haven't ever spoken to a medium before, but what you have told me tonight has helped me. Now I can continue with my life in the knowledge that I'll meet up with Jimmy once more—that he's safe and well and with people who love him as much as I do. What you've said is such a comfort to me and has proved to me that Jimmy is not lost.'

I breathed a sigh of relief. It was one of the most difficult situations I have ever had to deal with, but I was extremely pleased that I had been able to help Mary.

For the rest of the holiday I heard no more from Jimmy. My job was done and he was happy that Mary now knew that he still loved her deeply and would always care for her from the spirit realms.

ALL AT SEA

The sun was beating down as I lay sprawled on a sun lounger on the Lido deck with my eyes closed. Suddenly the sun disappeared as a body placed itself between me and it and a voice said, 'Hello! I'm sorry to bother you, but can I ask, are you Derek Acorah who's on television?'

I squinted up and saw that a young woman was standing over me. 'My name's Karen,' she said. 'Please forgive me for bothering you, but can I tell you that my family and I love your paranormal programmes and are great fans. I haven't approached you before, but I just couldn't leave it any longer!'

I knew that Karen was a nice person. I also knew that she was hurting deeply but I couldn't help feeling slightly irritated and resentful that once again the world of spirit were insisting that I continue working even though I was supposed to be on holiday!

Karen was beginning to look embarrassed that she had approached me. 'Don't worry,' I told her.

As I spoke to her I could sense a lady in spirit building up beside her. 'My name is Elizabeth,' she said, 'and Karen is my daughter. I passed to the spiritual realms because I had cancer of the kidneys which progressed to my lungs. I was in great pain but tried to keep it from my three daughters as I hated to see them upset. Tell her I'm totally free of pain now. Tell her that I am so happy and that I have been reunited with my little boy, Karen's brother.'

Elizabeth went on to tell me that she had been totally surprised to meet her mother, whom she had never known in her physical life, as she had been adopted. She also said that her father was very close to her on the heavenly side.

She told me that the reason why Karen was so upset was because she had been unable to get to the hospital before her mother had passed from this world into the next. Her two other daughters, Mary and Betty, had been there and this only served to make Karen feel even more guilty. 'Tell Karen that she must stop thinking and saying that she wants to join me,' she said.

I knew that it was important that I relay to Karen these messages of comfort and love from her mother. I looked up at her and related what her mother had said. I told her that she must stop all the feelings of guilt and remorse and that her mother wanted her to get on with her life and be happy. She had so much to live for and she must stop making herself feel so sad.

As I spoke I could see the dark burden of guilt and depression lifting almost miraculously from Karen. She thanked me and apologized once more for interrupting me.

'I was happy to help,' I smiled.

Later that evening, as I was strolling along the deck, I bumped into a man who tapped me on the arm and said, 'Derek! Thanks for helping my daughter Karen. It's ironical that Elizabeth chose you and these surroundings to come through to my girl. When I first met her she worked on the ships!'

I heard a chuckle in my ear. Elizabeth was back. 'And tell Peter that he's not changing his shirts often enough!' she said.

When I told him, Peter laughed. 'That's my Elizabeth,' he laughed as he shook my hand, 'always there right behind me!'

A Return to Liverpool
Football Club

I was 18 years of age when I last trod the hallowed turf of my favourite football club. It had been a warm day in May 1968 when I had cast a last long, lingering look over the ground which had been my home for nearly four years. On that day I had been feeling hurt and disappointed that my cherished ambition to become a member of the Liverpool Football Club first team had not been achieved and I was to move on to another football club.

Early in 2003 I had been contacted by Lace International. They had expressed a wish to produce a video covering my experiences as a spirit medium and had come up with the idea of taking me back to Liverpool Football Club to retrace my steps as a player for the team. What a fantastic experience that turned out to be.

On arrival at Anfield we were met by Brian Hall, an ex-Liverpool player and friend, who is now the community liaison officer at the club. Brian had not changed one bit. He laughed and joked as he took us around the greatest football club in the world (although I am being slightly biased here!).

I entered the ground through the players' tunnel, not forgetting to place a kiss on the badge overhead as I did so. After I had wandered around the perimeter for a while talking of my memories whilst playing with the club, I climbed the steps into one of the stands and sat down. As I gazed out over the perfectly groomed pitch I became aware that I was not alone. I had been joined by a man in spirit whom I immediately recognized as none other than Tom Bush, the ex-Liverpool player and coach. Tom used to travel around with the junior sides when I first signed as an apprentice and I well remembered his dapper style and the ever-present cigar hovering at the corner of his mouth.

Tom had something to say. He pointed out that 'the boss', Bill Shankly, was not at all pleased that the club was seriously considering relocating. He was also not at all keen on something that was happening at the Kop end of the ground, especially in and around the penalty box. I looked over to that area and could see a man on his knees doing something with a metal tool. I shouted over to Brian, told him what Tom was saying and asked what the workman was doing.

'*You* tell *me* what Tom is saying he's doing, Derek,' came Brian's flippant reply.

His face was an absolute picture of amazement when I told him that Tom was saying that the workman was threading strands of imitation grass into the bald areas of the penalty box.

'He's right!' he said. 'And no one apart from me, the chap doing the work and Mr. Houllier knows about this. I don't know what to say! That's crazy stuff, Derek!'

I stood up to have one last walk around the ground. As I walked onto the pitch, who was waiting for me but one of the funniest men still in and around the game of football: Sammy, the groundsman. One of the camera crew asked Sammy whether he remembered me from my days at the club.

'Of course I do! How could I forget young Derek? He was fast, you know—one of the fastest that we've had on our books! Faster than Michael Owen!' (I did mention that Sammy had an acute sense of humour!)

Sammy went on to recall all my old footballing mates— Lee Koo, Jimmy Bowman, Kevin Marsh, Peter Bruce, and of course my old Bootle Boys schoolmate and ex-Liverpool manager Roy Evans.

'Many things have changed over the years,' he said, but he was hopeful that the great years would be coming back. 'They will, won't they, Derek?' he asked.

'Of course they will, Sammy' I replied, 'but not just yet. Not this season anyway. But don't worry, Sammy, the glory days will come back whilst you're still here looking after things.'

'That'll do me, Degs,' he said, smiling.

As I left the pitch, I had gone no more than 30 or 40 feet around the perimeter path when I was impressed by the presence of a young energy. The spirit of a young man had joined me and although he seemed to be quite content and happy, there was a slight agitation in his voice as he communicated with me. I mentally asked him what his concern was and whether he wanted to communicate with me.

He told me that he was one of the people who didn't arrive home after that fateful day at Hillsborough, some 15 years earlier. He told me that although he had missed his family here on Earth, he had now got used to living in the world of spirit with family members who had passed before him. He said that he visited his earthly home regularly without his family members knowing it. 'What a pity none of them's a medium,' he laughed. 'That would be just perfect!' He had obviously retained his sense of humour and fun. 'It was nice speaking to you, Degs. Keep up the good work! Ta ra!'

Years earlier I had been consulted by many families whose loved ones had passed to spirit as a result of events on that terrible day. It had been one of the darkest days in footballing history and I had wept with the family members who came to visit me as they received proof of the continuance of life after physical death by communicating with their loved ones in spirit. As a mark of respect to these families I have always kept private the names and details and I continue to do so to this day. This is the reason why I have not named here the young man who communicated with me at Anfield.

It was time to go. Brian Hall escorted us to the front of Anfield. As we were standing beneath the statue of the great man 'Shanks' we all heard a shout. 'Derek! There's Derek! I can't believe it! It's Derek!'

We turned to see a lady running towards us. 'You won't remember me 'cos it's been 14 years,' she said, 'but I had a private reading with you and I've still got the tape at home. You said that I'd meet an Irishman named Michael from Belfast, that we'd fall in love and marry. I was beginning to lose hope, but eight years after the reading I met him. You even gave me his mother and father's name as extra proof.' Turning to a man who had joined her, she said, 'I'd like you to meet Michael Burke from Belfast.'

The man held out his hand to shake mine. 'Hello,' he said. 'At long last I've met you. Every time Bet sees you on the television she brings up the subject of the reading she had with you. I was always sceptical, but when I listened to the tape recording of Bet's sitting with you I had to change my mind.'

It had certainly been a day for memories!

I was to return once more to Anfield later in the year when I was requested by Liverpool Football Club's official website to take part in an interview and discussion. I was asked many questions about my feelings for Liverpool.

We progressed to some rather sensitive issues. 'How do you see Liverpool doing short term?' asked the interviewer. 'Any honours this year?'

I shook my head. 'Sorry—nothing!' I answered. 'What I have received from spirit is that I do not see Mr. Houllier here at Anfield as manager beyond the season of 2004.

I can see a very upbeat manager taking over who comes from a team who have been used to wearing striped shirts.'

We will all have to wait and see whether my prediction proves correct!

PSYCHOMETRY

Psychometry is the system of tuning in to the residual energy of an item, be it a piece of furniture, a painting, an item of jewelery, anything in fact which has been in the ownership of a person. The item will absorb the energies of that person and a psychometrist can pick up on those energies and give information pertaining to its ownership.

All mediums and psychics are capable of using psychometry. In fact anybody who is sensitive, with a little concentration, can tune in to the vibrations of an item and detect the circumstances surrounding the individuals who have had immediate contact with it.

The same rule applies to a building or other construction. Whilst travelling abroad I have been fortunate enough to visit such places as Pompeii, the Egyptian pyramids and the Mayan ruins. Upon touching the ancient stones I have been taken back to the times when these places were inhabited and have had wonderful experiences reliving the various cultures.

It is even possible to psychometrize a person. I have found that if a link between the spirit world and the querent is weak, by touching the person's hand my communication link with their spirit loved ones is greatly enhanced.

THE ANTIQUES GHOST SHOW

In October 2002 I was approached by Hilary Goldman of IPM Productions. She asked me whether I would be interested in taking part in a television programme which was to be called *The Antiques Ghost Show*. The format of the programme would be people bringing items for me to psychometrize. I would not to be allowed to meet the people or view the item until the cameras were rolling. I would be joined by two other people, Chris Gower and Anthony Adolph. Chris is an antiques expert. I had met him before whilst working for Granada Breeze. He had been another unfortunate victim when the television station closed down. The third member of the team, Anthony Adolph, is a genealogist. It would be his job to work on any information I could give that would help him to trace the family trees of the people who were bringing items along to the programme.

The idea appealed to me. It would make a pleasant change to meet people on a one-to-one basis once more.

On a blustery day in November I drove to Canterbury to meet the team and film a pilot programme. Within an hour or two of my arrival the first person had been ushered in to meet me. Chris and Anthony were at the ready, notebooks in hand, waiting to see what I could come up with.

There were a variety of objects to be psychometrized, ranging from coins to medals, from books to badges, and many items of jewelery. A lady brought in a mourning brooch. I was able to tell her that her forebears had made a hazardous journey from France by fishing boat in order to escape the French Revolution in the late 1780s. A gentleman brought in a pocket watch. I was able to tell him that the watch had been the property of a soldier who had been active in World War I and that he had probably been a pretty harsh personality.

By the end of the day I was exhausted and my head was buzzing with names and facts which had been contained in the residual energy of numerous family heirlooms. Anthony Adolph, who had confided to me that he was sceptical of mediumship, was later to write in a magazine article:

> I went into the project as a sceptic. In fact I thought it was the craziest thing I had ever heard in my life, and I was sure I would discover how Derek really came up with correct facts. However, even as we worked on the first episode... my firm belief in the non-existence of other worlds began to founder.

I drove home feeling quite pleased with what I had achieved. Just as I thought, I had enjoyed meeting people again and I was quite overcome by the welcome I had received.

The pilot programme aired just prior to Christmas 2002. In February 2003 I received word that I would be required in March to complete the filming of a series of programmes. I had been in Cornwall filming for the *Most*

Haunted series at Pengersick castle. As I drove along the M4 heading towards Essex I reflected on my experiences at Pengersick. It had not been at all as I had imagined—tall turrets and crenellated battlements. All Pengersick consisted of was a square tower, three stories high, and some outbuildings. I would certainly have missed it altogether if I hadn't recognized the vehicles parked outside the gateway.

I remembered dancing with the spirit of a young girl on the roof of the castle. She had lost her physical life tragically when she had overbalanced and plunged from the battlements to the ground. I smiled to myself as I recalled the vigils when we had been sent to sit in small tents within the grounds. There had been plenty of panicking, but not an awful lot of spirit activity!

I had reached the M25 and was soon heading off up the M11 towards Sawbridgeworth in Hertfordshire where I was to spend the next five days.

ONE BRAVE HEART

Again, the variety of family heirlooms was vast. There were brooches and books, swords and sticks, coins and whole cupboards! There was even a glass walking stick which upon first sight looked exactly like a sugar cane that you would see in a fairground.

Standing on the rear patio of the premises at which we were filming, I had been looking out over the Hertfordshire countryside when suddenly the whole scene changed. I was no longer viewing the lush green meadows but could see the arid brown lands of another continent. I was in

Africa. I could hear gunshots and the low, distant chant of an African tribe. 'Zulus!' Sam told me. 'What you can hear is the war chant of Zulu warriors.'

I wondered why I would be suddenly thrust into such a scenario. 'The next item will tell you,' Sam advised.

I was taken through to the front of the house and into the room where the programme was being filmed and Dave from Sheffield was introduced to me. He is a wrestler and glories in the professional name of 'The Iron Duke'. In front of him stood a large glass case which contained a model of the ship HMS *Marlborough*. Dave, Chris and Anthony took their seats and the filming began.

As I placed my hand on the glass case I was impressed to utter the words: 'One brave heart!' I was taken back clairvoyantly to the African landscape which I had experienced on the patio earlier. Again I could hear the crack of gunshot and the low insistent chanting which grew louder and louder. I heard the name 'Rorke's Drift' whispered to me by Sam and I could see a man in a uniform which had once been red and white.

'William's here,' I told Dave. 'He'd rather be called Billy. He was a courageous man who was fighting for his freedom. There were lots of deaths. There are warriors chanting but he's saying, "They'll not get me!" Many men went down, but he managed to save a few. He's talking about a name which sounds like "Ellen". He's telling me that there is something carved underneath the model of the ship.'

Dave looked stunned. The model that he brought along had been constructed by his great, great uncle, William

(Billy) Allen, who had been one of the last men left standing at Rorke's Drift. He had been awarded the VC for his efforts in saving a handful of men who had survived the massacre immortalized in the film *Zulu*, which starred Michael Caine. Billy Allen's daughter's name was Eleanor.

THAT SPOOKY THING...

There were many other items. Elaine brought along a smoking hat and I was able to tell her about the man who had a taste in oriental culture and who had played the banjo. Anne arrived carrying a painting which was discovered to be an original dating back to 1603. Upon touching the picture I was given the impression of a royal connection, of legal dealings and a coronation. Later we discovered that the painting depicted Sir Timothy Lowe, a lawyer, who had been knighted in the year of James I's accession to the throne.

Sharon and Rob brought along Rob's great uncle's travelling box. They were amazed when I gave them his name as William Slater and confirmed his sergeant's three stripes. Chris disagreed with my statement that William's chest had been used to house his belongings whilst he travelled the seven seas. He was of the opinion that the item was a linen chest. Later investigation proved that I was in fact correct.

Once filming was completed it was the turn of Chris and Anthony to spend the next few weeks scurrying around the country following up the information I had gleaned from all the items which had been brought in. It was with some trepidation that I made my way back to Essex a few weeks later to film their findings and to see whether the results of my psychometry had indeed tied in with the facts that they had uncovered. How foolish I would look if they hadn't!

However, I was to be pleasantly surprised. In fact I should have known that Sam would not let me down.

Now *Antiques Ghost Show* airs regularly in the UK and is also shown across Canada. 'We're big in Banff!' was the line Anthony e-mailed me with.

I was pleased and proud to meet up with some Canadian people when I was on holiday early in 2004. 'Hey, aren't you that guy off the television?' were the words they greeted me with. 'Don't you do that spooky thing with people's belongings?'

I suppose I had to agree with them, though I have never heard of the ancient art of psychometry being described in quite such a way before!

LOTTERY

Over the many years of my career as a medium I have been asked on numerous occasions to provide the winning numbers for the National Lottery. This, of course, is impossible for any medium to predict. The gift of mediumship is not to be used in such a manner. The work of a medium is to provide proof of life after physical death, not to make people rich!

It has happened, however, on one or two occasions during a private sitting that I have been shown a huge upturn in a querent's financial situation and have subsequently been told that they have indeed won large sums of money on the lottery or, on one occasion, the football pools. There was one incident, however, which involved neither the National Lottery nor the football pools, but the Grand National, the famous National Hunt event held at Aintree racecourse each spring. This is not a tale of what was—more a tale of what might have been!

THE GRAND NATIONAL

It was a Saturday morning and the Grand National was due to be run that afternoon. I had agreed to visit the home of a friend of mine to conduct a sitting for his wife.

Normally I would not have been working on a Saturday morning, but I was doing this as a special favour. My friend is a businessman in Liverpool and has many contacts in the racing world. It was inevitable therefore that on this day he would receive telephone calls offering tips for the winner of the Grand National.

After I had completed the sitting, I sat enjoying a cup of coffee as he discussed the merits or otherwise of the various contenders for the race.

'I'm afraid it's all wasted on me,' I told him. 'I'm not a gambling man.'

The telephone rang again. 'This is a dead cert,' my friend told me. 'It just can't lose, so why don't you put a couple of bob on it?'

I heard Sam chuckling in my ear. 'Little does he know, but that horse isn't going to win the Grand National. In fact there isn't going to be a winner this year!'

I was perplexed. As far as I knew the Grand National had been run at Aintree every year since it had begun. I could not see that today was going to be any different. The Thursday and Friday races had gone ahead as scheduled and apart from a shower of rain nothing untoward had taken place. But I could see Sam nodding sagely. 'The skies will be black, causing an enormous downpour,' he said, 'but that won't be the reason.'

I felt slightly put out at my spirit guide involving himself in the racing world. Nevertheless I repeated to my friend what he had just told me.

'Rubbish!' came the reply. 'I think you and Sam must be a bit tired!'

I laughed and agreed that that just might be the case.

Later that day curiosity drove me to turn on the television and watch the proceedings at Aintree. The time for the Grand National was drawing near. The sky over Liverpool was growing darker and darker and I ended up having to turn on the electric light in my home.

The horses lined up for the main event, the starting gate flew up, but a false start was declared. This happened once or twice more. When the race finally appeared to be underway and the horses were three or four fences in, people were running onto the course, causing the horses to shy and run off the track. The race was abandoned. Sam was right! There wasn't a winner!

Later that evening my friend telephoned me. 'I just don't believe it!' he said. 'If I had taken notice of you and Sam and put money on the race *not* being run, I'd be a millionaire!'

There has been one other occasion when I have involved myself in the Grand National. This was in the year 2003. A relative of mine had been joking with me for a number of weeks, asking me who was going to win the race. 'I don't know,' I said, 'but I do know that the jockey will be Irish and will be wearing green and purple silks with a star on the head covering. The initial "M" is relevant to the horse's name.'

On the morning of the Saturday when the Grand National was due to be run Gwen and I were returning from a *Most Haunted* location in Cumbria. We had stopped off in Windermere for a coffee and had bought the morning newspapers. Gwen was idly flicking through one of the tabloids and reached the centre pages, which showed the jockeys' colours.

One set of colours leaped off the page at me. 'That's the one!' I said, pointing to the page. 'That's the winning jockey!'

We arrived home just as the Grand National was about to begin. Sure enough, the horse and jockey I had chosen in Windermere romped home. Apparently it was far from being a favourite to win and it came as quite a surprise to everybody when it passed the winning post.

MONEY ISN'T EVERYTHING

There is one incident which proved to me that money luck does not always bring happiness.

I had been consulted by a lady named Irene. Everything had gone well in the sitting and I had been able to communicate with various members of her family who had passed to the world of spirit. One of these was her brother Jimmy. He had always been a gambling man during his time here on Earth and his tastes had obviously not changed since passing on to the higher side of life. 'Tell your Colin to give you a quid to buy a lottery ticket' was the last message he passed on to his sister. Colin was Irene's husband and he was against gambling in any form. Nevertheless, Irene promised her brother that she would obtain the necessary £1 coin from him and buy a ticket.

I thought no more about the reading until a few weeks later when I arrived at my office to find a huge bouquet of flowers and a box of luxury chocolates waiting for me. On the card attached to the flowers was written the words: 'Thanks, Derek! I hit the jackpot!' It was signed 'Irene'. I was most pleased that she had taken her brother's advice. Obviously he had been able to see good fortune in store for his sister and had known that the key to that good fortune was the purchase of a lottery ticket.

Some 12 months later, however, Irene arrived at my office once more. 'I had to come and see you again, Derek,' she said, 'because I'm so upset at what's happened.'

She proceeded to tell me that the previous year she had won the lottery jackpot of some £2.3 million. She was absolutely ecstatic and had vowed to improve the life of all her brothers and sisters by giving them £100,000 each to either buy a house or pay their existing mortgages off. She had also purchased a new house for her mother. Everybody had been very happy and her two brothers and three sisters had gone off to look for new homes. Her two brothers and two of her sisters found suitable houses, but her third sister could not find anything within her price range which pleased her. 'She wanted another £20,000,' Irene told me. She had agreed to give her sister the extra money, but when her other siblings had discovered this, a family feud had erupted. They all wanted more money. To add to the problems, Irene's mother had passed to the world of spirit and now the home that Irene had bought her was the subject of more arguments.

Irene was heartbroken. Her kind gesture had caused nothing but problems. 'I just wish that I hadn't won the damned money,' she said. Her husband Colin had advised her to leave them all to it, but it was difficult for her. She was very close to her brothers and sisters, especially as both their parents were now in the spirit world.

This sad story proves that money is not everything. Sometimes having it can cause more problems than not having it. People can become greedy and lose sight of the fact that a close and loving family is worth more than all the money in the world.

MEETING MY
SPIRIT GUIDE

Although we all have a main spirit guide or guardian, as some people call them, who is designated at our birth into this physical life, we also have helpers and other spiritual beings who touch upon our lives at various times when we are undertaking various experiences. They may come in to help us through difficult times or to inspire us when decisions have to be made. These guides and helpers may be members of our families who have passed to the world of spirit before us or they may be people who had expertise in certain subjects in their physical lives and have decided that they will spend some of their time in the spirit world helping us through the trials and tribulations of our daily lives here on Earth. Many spiritual healers, for example, have guides who were doctors in their earthly incarnation.

Many of you will be familiar with Sam my spirit guide, having seen and heard me converse with him on television and radio. Sam has also been close by my side during investigations into haunted locations throughout the UK. I have been asked on numerous occasions how it happened that I have Sam as my spirit guide, how we met and how we became so close.

The story begins over 2,000 years ago when I was incarnated as a member of a family who lived in Ethiopia. My family were very poor farmers. I was one of five children, having two brothers and two sisters. We were all expected to help my mother and father to scratch a living from the barren Ethiopian land in which we lived. I, however, was a rebel even then and often used to wander off on my own.

In those days many travellers used to pass through our village. One of these was well known to us all, as he would frequently return. His name was Masumai. He used to speak to the villagers of times of change, of why we were all here on this Earth and of what was expected of us. It became evident to me even at my young age that he was blessed with special gifts, gifts which neither my father nor my mother possessed.

Although we were peaceful people, at times feuds would occur. One awful day a large group of men invaded our village. There was much screaming and shouting and some homes were set alight. Many people were killed, my mother, father, brothers and sisters amongst them. I escaped harm because I had wandered a short distance from the village. When I heard the noise of battle I hid in some bushes on the outskirts. When the noise subsided and night fell I crept back to my home, which had escaped the fires of the invaders. I was alone and terrified. For the first time in my life I had no one. I was also very tired and hungry, and mortally afraid that the invaders would return. My nine-year-old eyes had witnessed so much, but eventually exhaustion took over and I slept.

I awoke in the morning and felt once more the shock of isolation. Creeping out, I managed to find a few scraps of food and a little water. Gathering these together, I fled back to my home and piled some wood behind the door to prevent anybody opening it from the outside. I stayed there on my own for three days.

On the fourth day I heard a loud noise outside and someone shouting my name over and over. It was Masumai. I ran to him, crying uncontrollably. He put his arm around me and held me close whilst I relayed to him what had happened to our village. He listened and held me tenderly whilst he calmed me down. Despite my sorrow I felt uplifted. I was no longer alone.

Masumai explained to me that my family were beyond hurt now, that they were in a world where no harm could come to them and that one day I would be reunited with them. He told me that until that time came he would be a father to me.

After that day Masumai and I left the village. We walked to places I had never heard of, relying on the people of the villages to offer food and simple shelter to us in return for Masumai's guidance. Weeks, months and years of being with Masumai, listening to him talking to people in far-off regions of Ethiopia, afforded me a deeper understanding of this great yet simple man. He told me that one day I would be like him, but not yet, as I was only 13 years old.

Months passed and we found ourselves in an area which was unknown even to Masumai. He told me that we would have to be careful in our approach. We discovered that the people were not very friendly and had no regard for Masumai's teachings, and decided that we should move on. We both felt that these people could be similar to those who had attacked my village four years earlier.

We carried on walking until we reached a small hill with some bushes which we felt would provide some cover for us for the night. We were both very hungry. Masumai asked me to find some small pieces of wood so that we could light a fire and at least be warm. I moved further and further away until I reached the edge of the village through which we had passed earlier. Although I knew it was wrong to steal, I thought of how hungry and tired Masumai had looked and how much he had helped me and cared for me. I crawled very slowly up to a window ledge where loaves of bread were cooling, grabbed a small loaf and crawled away.

I was almost back to the place where Masumai and I had set up camp for the night when I heard shouting. Before I knew it, I was surrounded by a circle of men. I felt a harsh pain in my side and then in my leg and fell down. I felt as though I was falling backwards as I lost consciousness. My attackers, thinking I was dead, left and returned to their village.

The next thing I remember is hearing the voice I loved and trusted. Masumai was holding me close in his arms and crying, his tears falling onto my chest. I told him not to cry but to look in my clothes, as there was bread hidden there. He tried to stem the flow of blood from my wounds, but he knew that he could not save me. He told me that I would have to come back to a new life and that when the time arrived he would be by my side. He would be my guiding influence from the heavenly side because by that time he too would have undertaken the journey I was about to make. He told me that the stealing of the bread had been a spiritual act because I had not stolen it for myself but to help another. 'But,' he said, 'there is a payment to be made for all things!'

THE REUNION

Many years passed and after the end of my football career and my first marriage I was at a crossroads in my life.

It was at this point that Sam came back to me one evening when I was at home alone. We talked long into that night and he explained to me that the impressions and images that I had been receiving regarding my past life in Ethiopia were flashbacks to the time gone by when we had travelled together.

And why 'Sam' and not 'Masumai'? The reason is simple: it is Sam's wish that he be known by that name and not by the ancient name of 'Masumai'. He knew that I would be reincarnated into a white Western world and would not go back to the country where we first met. And he also knew that he would fulfil the promise he had made to me 2,000 years earlier.

TREADING THE BOARDS

I have now been appearing in large theatres throughout the UK for many years. I am not on my own, of
course. There are many mediums filling theatres, perhaps
the two best known being my good friends Colin Fry and
Tony Stockwell.

Colin, Tony and I first met and worked together on stage
demonstrating to a studio audience for a LIVINGtv programme titled *The Three Mediums*. We went on to appear at the
Hammersmith Apollo in June 2003, where we demonstrated
mediumship to an audience of 3,000 people. I often think
back in amazement to the days when an audience could con-
sist of only a handful of people. Who would have thought
that three ordinary men would have people queuing up to see
them demonstrate their gifts? The word of spirit is definitely
being spread every day now!

When I go to a theatre I am obviously unaware of the
people who will be coming to see me. All I can do is rely on
Sam not to let me down and to be there to give me messages

to pass on to members of the audience. Maybe loved ones belonging to those audience members will come along from the world of spirit and allow me to talk to their sons, daughters, husbands, wives, or in fact anybody they may have known whilst they lived in this physical world.

AN OLD FRIEND

On one occasion during a theatre show just outside Liverpool, I was surprised to be joined on stage by someone who I knew rather well. Roger was a regular client of mine in the days of my consulting room in Liverpool. He would come to see me once a year and I would conduct a reading for him. He had worked hard and had opened his own courier business, which was slowly growing. He had a good wife and a lovely son and daughter who were both in their teens. Each time he came to see me I would tell him that there were no particular changes for him. His working life was progressing and his home life was good. 'I love coming to see you, Derek,' he would say, 'because it's just brilliant to have a chat with my old mum and dad once a year!'

Roger's mother and father had both passed over to the world of spirit some years earlier. He was a true believer in the world beyond, but liked to hear from his parents during his visits to see me.

His last visit to my office was just prior to Christmas some years ago. As he was leaving I said to him, 'Do me a favour, Roger. Don't do any driving on Christmas Day.'

'No chance of that Derek,' he said. 'If anything needs carrying I pay people to do it for me now. I'll be sitting in front of the telly with my feet up!'

The years went by but I did not hear from Roger again. As each Christmastime approached I wondered whether he would call me up to see me, but I heard nothing. Maybe he had decided that he no longer wanted to have a sitting, or maybe he had found another medium he preferred to consult.

Now Christmas was approaching and I was scheduled to appear at a theatre not too far away from Liverpool. I had been on stage demonstrating for about 30 minutes when I heard a voice coming from the world of spirit that I recognized. It was Roger. As his spirit form built up beside me he said to me, 'I know, I know, Derek! You did warn me! My wife Rita and my daughter Linda are in the audience. I'd like you to tell them that I'm OK and that I love them and Peter. I'm looking out for them and I'll always be around them.'

He reminded me of the last time that he had come to see me in my office when I had asked him not to drive on Christmas Day. 'Would you believe it, Derek? In the morning I received a phone call telling me that my driver was ill and couldn't make a very important delivery. I had to do the job myself. I forgot all about your warning. I got into the van and set off down the M6. I'd not gone very far when another driver lost control and slammed into me. My van rolled and I didn't come out of it. I didn't think I'd ever be talking to you from this side!'

I passed on Roger's messages of love to Rita and Linda. They were delighted to hear from him and greeted my message with tears of joy.

'What a pity,' I thought, 'that such a lovely man had to pass to spirit so early in his physical life.' He was only 41 years of age. I knew that he was sincere in his message, though. Knowing Roger as I did I was certain that he would care for his family from spirit side just as he had when he was with them physically.

'HAVE I BEEN DREAMING?'

One morning I was downloading my e-mails and came to one which really made me sit up and take notice. A gentleman named Ralph Jones from Newcastle wrote that he had a very interesting story to tell, but before he would explain everything he desperately required a personal reading with me. I sensed that he was very anxious and replied to him explaining that because I lived in Southport and he lived in Newcastle, a personal reading would prove impossible until I was in his area conducting a demonstration.

Later in the day I checked my diary and discovered that I would be appearing in the Newcastle area later that year. I e-mailed Ralph and advised him of this fact. He replied immediately telling me that he was a little disappointed at the length of time he would have to wait, but he accepted that this was the only way things could be worked out.

Two months later I was in Newcastle. After a show I always stay behind to meet the people who have come along to see me. After I had finished signing autographs, a gentleman approached me. 'Derek, I'm so pleased to see you at last. I'm Ralph.'

I asked whether he had enjoyed the evening and he replied that he had very much. He told me that he was totally intrigued and that it was both fascinating and reassuring to hear the messages passed on from people in the world of spirit to their loved ones in the audience.

'Considering the way that I was thinking about your work, it has totally blown me away,' he said. 'I have to be very honest with you—I have been a sceptic virtually all my adult life.'

I told him that that was perfectly alright, that people were entitled to their own views and I accepted that not everybody could accept my beliefs.

I took Ralph back to my dressing room to conduct the personal reading I had promised. 'I sincerely hope that this reading helps you and that you will receive the advice and contact with loved ones which you are seeking,' I said to him.

The first insight I received slightly rocked me. I saw Ralph in a lorry driving along a road. The picture then changed. Ralph was still in the cab of the lorry, but now he was slumped over the driving wheel. I could see blue flashing lights and an ambulance. Ralph was receiving medical attention. There were tubes connected to him and it looked as though a medic was attempting to give heart massage.

Ralph was staring at me fixedly. 'I can't believe this, Derek. Please go on,' he said.

My insights were coming thick and fast. Now I was clairvoyantly viewing Ralph in a hospital bed. Doctors and nurses were working frantically. A man said, 'We've lost him. I'm afraid he's gone!'

My eyes were fixed on an apparently lifeless figure on a bed. The doctors and nurses had gone, but there was a lady standing next to the bed stroking Ralph's head. I was impressed by the name 'Alice'.

I asked Ralph whether he understood any of this. He said that it was as though I was taking the pictures directly from his mind. I quietly told him that it was not mind reading. As far as I am concerned, there is no such thing as mind reading.

I felt as though I had experienced a massive heart attack. I mentioned this to Ralph. He moved his chair and said that all I had said in the reading was true and accurate.

At this point the spirit form of a lady began to build next to me. 'I'm Alice,' she told me. 'I love Ralph very much and always will. He misses me so much since I passed over to the world of spirit.'

She went on to tell me that she had been ill for quite some time before she had passed over and that Ralph had cared for her very lovingly. At the time of his heart attack she had been beside him. She wanted him to know that he was not coming to join her and other family members just yet. She explained that one of the main reasons Ralph wanted this reading was to confirm what he had seen when the doctors had given up and thought that they had lost him.

Ralph listened intently to all that I had to say. 'You've answered virtually everything I needed to know,' he said, 'and have confirmed the most important thing which means more to me than life itself.'

Ralph had been driving his lorry on his daily run when he began to experience tremendous pains in his chest. He felt that he must have become unconscious because when he came round he could see lots of people leaning over him. He heard a voice telling him to 'hold on' and then he thought he must have been dreaming because he saw his wife Alice holding his hand telling him that she was fine and that he was going to hospital. She told him she would go with him and that he should not be afraid.

He then said that he must have been awake for a little while because he had noticed that he was in a room. There were lots of people in white coats talking and doing things around him then suddenly everything went dark. He saw Alice coming towards him and remembered asking her to take him with her, but she had replied, 'Ralph, you can't come with me yet. You have to get well.'

He told her that he felt fine, but then she pointed out to him that he was out of his physical body and told him to look over to the bed. When he did so, he remembered saying, 'Oh my God! That's me, isn't it?'

Alice nodded and told him that he had to go back, as it was not time for him to join her.

The next thing everything was going dark and then Ralph was waking up to see the doctors all frantically moving about the room. He heard a lady's voice shouting that his eyes had opened and that his vital signs were building. Some days later he was told that as far as the doctors were concerned he had been clinically dead but had somehow come back.

Ralph recovered well, but the one thing that he could not understand was the 'dream' when he thought he had seen and spoken to his wife. That was why he was so anxious to speak to me. He wanted to know whether in fact he had been dreaming or whether Alice had indeed been at his side that day. I explained that for a short time he had left his physical body and he had indeed briefly met up with Alice once more.

Ralph sat and reflected on his reading. 'I know now that my lovely wife is still alive,' he said, 'maybe in another place, but she lives on. I also know that I did leave my body because I saw with my own eyes my physical body on the bed. The medical people have told me that I died for a short while. I'll go now and God willing, will carry on in my life until it is my time for my Alice to come and collect me. My scepticism has been banished forever.'

He told me that only a few evenings previously he had smelled a fragrance which he recognized as Alice's perfume. He had not seen her, but he had known that she was around him.

At this moment Alice reappeared in the room with us. She told me that before she had passed to the world of spirit she had placed a magnetized plaque on the door of their refrigerator at home. Written on it was a short prayer. She had noticed that Ralph had removed it. Ralph confirmed that this was true. Alice had bought the plaque and placed it on the door of the refrigerator nearly five years previously.

'Thank you from the bottom of my heart,' he told me as I left the dressing room. 'I will never forget what you have done for me.'

A MYSTERY

I had completed four shows in and around Scotland and this was my last day in Glasgow. During the afternoon I was sitting in a coffee shop with Gwen enjoying a café latte. I got up to pay the bill and when I returned I found that Gwen was talking to a lady who had sat down at our table.

'This is Mary,' Gwen told me. 'She watches all your programmes.'

I shook hands with Mary and said that I was very pleased to meet her. She told me that she had been to my show the previous evening but unfortunately she had not received a message. 'Not that it matters,' she added hastily 'It was wonderful just to watch you work and I do understand that no medium could get a message to all 1,200 people in two hours. Can I be cheeky and ask you a question, Derek?' She looked at me expectantly. It would have been churlish of me to refuse.

Mary explained that over the last three or four months she had been having some strange experiences. Each night when she retired to bed, just as she settled herself in with a book, she would suddenly hear tapping noises coming from the direction of the wardrobe. She had taken no notice, thinking that it was just the wood creaking, until one night just recently when no sooner had the tapping noises begun than to her amazement a light appeared. This light had started off as a speck but then grown and grown into a large ball of light and energy.

'I don't mind telling you, it scared the life out of me,' Mary said. 'I threw the covers over my head—I was scared to look at the thing!'

After five or ten minutes Mary had raised the covers from her head. What she saw then shocked her even more. There in front of her was a lady staring straight at her. Mary shouted out loud, 'Who are you? What do you want with me? I don't know you. Please go away!'

Since then the same thing had occurred night after night. Mary would be just settling down in bed when the apparition would appear.

A coffee shop in the middle of town is not the ideal place to conduct a reading, but I told Mary that I would try to help her. I opened myself to the influence of the world of spirit and was told by Sam that a lady in spirit was close by. This lady had been trying very hard to communicate with Mary, but had only succeeded in frightening her.

I then became aware of the spirit lady herself. I could see that she was about 40 years of age. She had dark hair, was of a slim build and was quite pretty. Sam told me that she was Mary's mother. She had not meant to frighten or shock her daughter. She had merely been trying to show herself to Mary for the first time since she had passed to the world of spirit. She had been most frustrated when she realized that although she had succeeded in allowing Mary to see her, she had been unable to communicate with her to let her know who she was.

I passed the information on to Mary, who sat looking rather stunned. 'I don't know what to say to you, Derek,' she said, 'because unless something drastic has happened, my dear old mum's at home, probably with her feet up watching the television. She had a slight stroke this time last year and of course takes medication, but she's still very much in the land of the living!'

I felt absolutely terrible. I was shocked at what Mary had to say and equally shocked at the thought that Sam could mislead me. I could still hear Sam conversing quietly with the spirit lady in the background. 'Ask her for some proof and more evidence of herself,' I desperately pleaded with him.

Sam proceeded to relay to me a very sad story. The lady in spirit had been just 16 when she had fallen pregnant. Her family was very religious and had disowned her. They could not stand the shame of their daughter giving birth to a baby out of wedlock. She had travelled to another town where she had given birth to Mary in a home for un-married mothers. She had been in no position to bring up the child, as apart from being only very young herself, she had no job or prospect of earning a living, and so she had been forced to give her up for adoption. Mary was taken away and she did not see her again. At last she managed to find a job as a housemaid and eventually met and married a man who was somewhat older than herself. They had moved away from Scotland and had lived quite happily in England. She regrettably had been unable to have further children. In her thirty-seventh year she had succumbed to breast cancer.

As I informed Mary of all this, I watched cautiously for her reaction. 'Oh, and there's one more thing,' I added. 'The lady says that Jean and Tom were good people.'

Mary's eyes widened. 'What names did you just say?' she asked.

I repeated the names 'Jean' and 'Tom'.

Mary explained that Jean and Tom were the names of her mother and father, but as she had said before, they were both still alive.

The mystery was growing deeper. Sam told me that the lady was saying that her name was Jenny and she had no wish to hurt Mary in any way. She just wanted her to know that her true blood mother loved her. At this point Mary said that she would like to go home to ask her mother and father a few questions. She asked whether she could make contact with me by letter or telephone. I told her that she could, as I would be interested to find out the answer to the riddle.

The following evening the telephone rang and it was Mary. 'I just had to get in touch with you to let you know,

Derek,' she said. She proceeded to tell me that she had gone straight to her mother's home. She had wondered how she could approach such a delicate subject, but finally had plucked up the courage to ask whether she had been adopted. Her mother had broken down and told her that she and Mary's father loved her so much that they had never been able to admit to her that she had in fact been adopted. They realized as Mary grew older that they had made a mistake in not being entirely honest with her, but as time had gone on, they just did not know how to approach the subject.

Mary's mother asked her how she had found out. Who had told her? Mary told her the story and her mother confirmed that her birth mother had been named Jenny—Jenny Brown.

Mary did not know whether to laugh or cry. 'It appears that I've got two mums now,' she said, 'one in spirit and one here whom I love dearly. I have one question to ask you, though, Derek: when it's my time to pass on, will I have to choose which mum I will be with?'

I told her that she would have the chance to be with both her mothers and that because of their equal love for her, Jenny and Jean would become very close.

'Thank you, Derek,' said Mary. 'I'm glad that I found out now and not when it was too late.'

MR. BOOKER

One of the most exciting incidents I have experienced whilst demonstrating on stage occurred in late 2003. I was

appearing at a theatre in Blackpool. It was the last engagement of a grueling autumn tour and the theatre was full to
capacity. I had been on stage for approximately 30 minutes
and was speaking to a member of the audience when suddenly I became aware of a gentleman in spirit who was
standing almost in the wings to the right of me. He was
chuntering and muttering and occasionally shouting in an
attempt to draw my attention to him.

'Would you just wait a moment?' I asked him. 'I'm
speaking at the moment, but I will announce you shortly.'

I continued with my communication, but the spirit man
refused to give up. 'My name's Mr. Booker and I want to
speak to Mark,' he shouted. 'He's up there!' He pointed to
the upper circle.

I asked him once again to be kind enough to wait whilst
I continued with the reading I was doing. At that, he
stamped around a little. He was obviously an impatient
soul and was not prepared to allow me to finish speaking.

Whilst on stage I always have a small table which holds
a jug of water and a couple of glasses. As I continued
speaking I heard a gasp from the audience. 'Look, Derek!
Look at the glass!' some people shouted.

Turning to look at the table, I could see the man in
spirit pushing the glass along the surface. 'Stop that!' I
shouted to him, but too late. The glass toppled over the
edge and fell onto the stage. There was a stunned silence.

'Don't do that again!' I commanded. 'If you do, I won't
announce you to your loved ones and I will ask Sam to
take you to the back of the queue!'

The spirit man was unrepentant. 'I want to speak to Mark,' he demanded once more. 'I'm his grandfather.'

'Is there a Mark Booker sitting in the upper circle?' I asked the audience. A hand shot up from that area. 'Your grandfather's here,' I announced. 'He wants to speak to you. He's very impatient, but I will come to you in a moment.'

Yet again I attempted to continue with the earlier communication, but Mr. Booker was not prepared to allow this. There was another gasp from the audience and one or two people shouted again. I turned once again, just in time to see the second glass being propelled towards the edge of the table. Once again, the glass toppled over, rolled off the stage and crashed down onto the floor below. Once more there was a stunned silence from the audience.

'I'm so sorry, Derek,' called out Mark.

As his grandfather was obviously not prepared to wait, I relented and passed on the messages I was receiving both from him and from Mark's other grandfather, Tom, who was also in spirit.

I later received an e-mail from Mark apologizing for his grandfather's actions and explaining as follows:

Thank you for connecting with my two granddads on Thursday night at the Grand Theatre in Blackpool. Both my wife and I needed to know that our 11-year-old son was being watched over and that message came through loud and clear. My granddad Mr. Booker passed over early in 1999 and the last four years of his life were spent in a nursing home. He was not able to get out of bed and was not able to communicate very well.

Some spirit people can be extraordinarily determined to get their messages across to their loved ones here on Earth, and Mr. Booker was one of them. His message was necessary and he was aware of that necessity. But I only hope that the next time he communicates through a medium, they are using a plastic beaker!

AFTERWORD

*N*ow the fourth and fifth series of *Most Haunted* are in the process of being filmed. Who knows what experiences this will bring? Will the team capture paranormal activity on film? Will a spirit entity decide not to be camera shy and show itself to the nation so that people can see what I can see—what I take for granted as a normal part of my everyday life? Who knows? We will have to wait to find out.

My theatre tours continue and this year I am treading the boards countrywide. Am I enjoying myself? Of course I am! And I know that my work for spirit will continue in whatever way is meant until the day arrives when I, too, will make that final journey to my home in the spirit world.